THE
ABARA
RANCH
COOKBOOK

Kent Trebilcox

THE STOVEARTS PRESS

THE

ABARA
RANCH

COOKBOOK

The A Bar A Cookbook. Copyright © 1996 by Kent Trebilcox. Printed and bound in the United States Of America. All rights reserved. No part of this book may be reproduced in any form or by any electronic or mechanical methods including, but not limited to, storage and/or retrieval systems without permission in writing by the publisher. The only exception is by reviewers who may use or quote short passages in their review. Published by the StoveArts Press, Box 7013, Charlottesville, Virginia 22906.

Library of Congress Catalog Card Number: 96-92322
ISBN 0-9652811-0-8

This book was prepared on the Macintosh. The types are Palatino and Jimbos™ from Intecsas.

Cover photo and illustrations by Kent Trebilcox
Graphic design by Deborah Chappell Benz
Jeans by Brooks

Acknowledgments

I wish to thank all of my loyal friends and supporters who have given me the encouragement to proceed with this project. There have been many wonderful people over the years who chose to work in the kitchen at the A Bar A, and I thank all of them.

My warmest thanks goes to ranch managers Bob and Margie Howe who have steadfastly supported me in all times.

The A Bar A magic is largely a result of the dedication and love of Mr. Charles Gates, who with the members of his family saw the vision of such a place and made the vision a reality.

'Muchas Gracias' to the famous El Presidente of Los Huevos Rancheros, Angelo Economou and to Jackie, who keep my star alight in the sky, so I always have someplace higher to aim for.

This book is dedicated to my creative director, editor, agent and love of my life, Brooks Morrison, whose unfailing confidence, great judgment and support saw me through.

Thank you.

For
MAX and TIARE

Table of Contents

Introduction

When I first came to the A Bar A Ranch in 1989 I had no experience with the 'Dude Ranch' experience. As the new chef, I inherited the responsibility of providing well prepared meals to a wide variety of guests from all over the world who shared something: discerning taste.

The A Bar A represents the best in many ways and the food I was to provide needed to fit the bill. Because the majority of our customers return year after year we are cautious with major changes. I had to ease them gently into a new style of food. It was no less a task than changing the brand of our bath soap. It would definitely be noticed!

My first goal was to include the previous chef's 'meat and potatoes' format into my broader repertoire which included lighter choices and the freshest ingredients. In order to succeed I needed the help of creative purveyors from around the country to provide the quality products necessary to realize my goal.

In the process, I was introduced to organically grown produce. Initially it was the organics' superior taste that attracted me and furthermore the nature of the farming and the farmers themselves shared the same commitment to quality as the A Bar A. Our first steps were tentative but they soon became excited leaps as we noticed just how special organic foods were. Our guests responded with great enthusiasm so in two years I was buying 90% organic, including flours, grains and many dairy products. Among our purveyors nationwide we are well known for expecting the finest, a reputation we share with our guests.

I offered traditional Ranch fare... also Mexican, Italian, French, Asian... all with spontaneity. I've never been one to plant my roots in any culinary landscape long enough for food critics to categorize my work. This has its disadvantages but fortunately our generous guests have learned to appreciate the element of surprise.

The most difficult part of this plan is repeating the successes. That's the true purpose of a recipe. While I do respect the need for them, I don't usually follow them exactly as they were intended. That is a curse of the food professional.

Albert Jorant, my chef-professor at the Cordon Bleu in Paris proudly and eagerly offered his recipes developed over five decades in the kitchen. He often said, with smirking wisdom, that a recipe in the hands of several people would result in many different outcomes. His theory stuck with me and I've depended rather softly on defined cooking guidelines ever since.

Soon enough I was faced with the challenge of training a staff of inexperienced college students in a system where formal recipes didn't exist and the standards were high. Previously my view of on the job training meant reforming and directing a cook's existing skills. Now I didn't have any skills to direct. I took a long look at square one.

I began with time consuming show-and-tell marathons that tried the limits of patience. Eventually I decided the best teaching method was the use of the printed word. After all, these were students...they could relate to paper. It wasn't an immediate conversion because I hung onto my stubborn habits, first only lazily writing down some recipes. I would casually list some or most of the ingredients. Sometimes they even included quantities. These early recipes were filled with notations, adjustments and substitutions... not much help.

I was eventually persuaded to apply some definition to my recipe writing due to our many guests' requests. They most certainly tired of my explanation that we didn't have recipes per se. I'm sure they thought I was being coy or worse yet, untruthful. I still have unfilled recipe orders that I hope can be satisfied with this collection.

While I've always respected the sage advise of my cynical professor back in France, he proposed a challenge. When can a Master artisan no longer feel threatened by openly sharing the methods of his craft? And when does this energy shift from the possession of wisdom to the sharing of secrets? While the art of Chef Jorant was inimitable, as students, his teaching moved us to further the exploration beyond him. He placed in us some of his grace which is generosity. Moreover, he was dedicated to a higher virtue - the growth and enrichment of his students.

Several years ago while young and impressionable I was working in a Denver restaurant with a 'seasoned' chef named Andy. On the menu was a very popular chocolate MudPie. After making a dozen of them almost daily for months I had become so unconscious with that repetitive task that when asked years later to prepare a Mudpie for my employer, Colorado Governor Richard Lamm... I couldn't recall the recipe. I managed to find Andy's telephone number. He was now retired and hopefully the possessor of the recipe I needed. After cordial greetings and a bit of catching up, I innocently asked him for the recipe. There was a long pause, then he started on about the cold winter and something about how therapeutic a month's vacation in Florida would be. I agreed, of course, then repeated my request. To my surprise he bluntly stated that he'd give me the recipe in exchange for a vacation to somewhere much warmer than Denver! Shocked and under considerable pressure to come up with a chocolate pie I scoured my memory. I vaguely recalled that the origin of this prized recipe had been a very loyal customer, Nancy Dick, at the time a State Legislator from Aspen and she had shared the coveted formula with the restaurant's owner whom she knew as a friend. But now she just happened to be the present Lieutenant Governor so I procured the recipe through diplomatic channels and successfully served a MudPie at the Governor's Mansion.

The challenge proposed by Chef Jorant together with the many recipe requests made by our guests at the A Bar A convinced me to redefine my role. Although flying by the seat of my pants has been mostly successful, it was impractical to teach from a disorganized volume of recipes stored in my mind. My staff often felt frustrated trying to devine my vaguely described concept of perfection. It is time to wrestle the book out and transcribe it. It should make room for new ideas, or another book... a mental garage sale, if you will.

This is in not a definitive work, but rather a pause along the way, a work in progress. This is a small collection, the results of spontaneous experiments performed for our gracious guests. I hope very much that within these pages one might find a small touch of that special A Bar A magic.

CHAPTER ONE

Starters

Sweet Red Pepper Soup with Saffron

When the late summer abundance of sweet, shiny red peppers overflow the markets and roadside produce stands, it's time to put up roasted peppers and make this rich, aromatic soup.

I would always tag along with my mother and grandmother as they shopped for bushels of ripe peppers from the truck farmers along Wisconsin's country roads, where I grew up.

Soon our entire house would fill with the sweet smell of charred pepper skins and fruity olive oil as they skillfully packed jars with layers of roasted and meticulously peeled peppers. Our weekend's toil was fully rewarded with a full winter's worth of sweet and crunchy *peperoni* for pasta, bruschetta, crostini and frittata.

FOR EIGHT SERVINGS

2 cups peeled, seeded, and diced
  red peppers, page 103
1 cup chopped leeks
3 tablespoons minced garlic
1 tablespoon olive oil
2 quarts chicken, veal or
  vegetable stock

¾ cup baby rice cereal
2 teaspoons kosher salt
⅛ teaspoon saffron threads
¾ cup heavy cream

TIED IN CHEESECLOTH

3 inch sprig rosemary
4 bay leaves

FOR THE GARNISH

¼ cup Italian parsley leaves
¼ cup red pepper brunoise

In a heavy soup pot cook the leeks and garlic in the olive oil until soft. Add the peppers, stock and rice cereal.

Stir in the saffron, then add the salt and the herbs.

Bring to a gentle simmer, while stirring. Cook for 30 minutes.

Remove the herbs in cheesecloth. Puree the soup in a blender or a food processor. Return it to the pot, add the cream and bring to a simmer.

Garnish with finely julienned leaves of Italian parsley mixed with a brunoise of fresh red pepper.

Eggplant Salad with Sweet Red Pepper Vinaigrette

FOR EIGHT SERVINGS

2 medium eggplant

semolina flour

3 beaten eggs

⅓ cup water

½ teaspoon kosher salt

½ teaspoon oregano

olive oil

FOR THE DRESSING

¾ cup diced roasted red peppers

1 teaspoon minced garlic

1 tablespoon minced shallot

¼ cup chopped Italian parsley

⅓ cup red wine vinegar

½ cup olive oil

1 teaspoon kosher salt

1 tablespoon sugar

½ teaspoon black pepper

2 tablespoons jumbo capers

¼ cup Italian parsley leaves

PREHEAT THE OVEN TO 350°

EQUIPMENT NEEDED

11"x 17"x 1" Baking sheet

Beat the eggs with water, salt and oregano. Slice the eggplant ⅛ inch thick. Quickly pass the eggplant slices through the egg mixture then into the semolina flour. Place them on a well oiled baking sheet and bake them until they are browned. Turn the slices to brown the other side. Set the cooked eggplant aside and repeat with all the slices, adding oil as needed.

Put all the dressing ingredients except the oil in a food processor. Blend well then add the olive oil while pulsing. Pour the dressing over the cooled eggplant and toss gently to coat. Arrange the slices on a serving platter and marinate for 2 hours before serving at room temperature. Garnish with the jumbo capers and parsley leaves.

Crema Milanese

My relationship with this wonderful soup was forged early in my life--on those difficult days when the need to go to school was successfully challenged by the urge to hide under the covers, feign an illness of uncertain description and settle into a day of watching television. Having bought the ruse, my mother would prepare this comforting remedy which I always recognized from the unmistakable aroma of browning butter. It remains a genuine favorite and has gained many new friends in recent years. It tastes better with Andy Griffith Show reruns.

MAKES FOUR - SIX SERVINGS
6 tablespoons butter
6 tablespoons flour

4 cups chicken stock, page 106
⅓ cup acine de pepe pasta
[substitute orzo or couscous]
2 teaspoons sea salt [none if canned broth is used]
¾ cup parmesan cheese

Cook the butter in a heavy saucepan until the foam subsides and it begins to lightly brown. The aroma smells like toasting nuts. Stir in the flour and cook two minutes over low heat. Off the heat add the stock while whisking. Bring to a simmer and add the pasta and salt. Stir often while cooking until the pasta is done. Serve with freshly grated parmesan cheese.

Bruschetta Rustica

Traditional bruschetta is made with a coarse grained rustic bread like Ciabatta, or slipper bread. Good quality, freshly baked Italian or French bread will work well or even focaccia can be used for a creative twist.

SERVES SIX - EIGHT
8 six inch open-face Ciabatta
½ cup olive oil
2-3 large garlic cloves
1 cup pesto, page 53
⅓ cup rehydrated sundried tomatoes
½ teaspoon black pepper
½ teaspoon sea salt
1 pound diced, fresh mozzarella cheese
⅓ cup chopped oil cured olives
2 teaspoons fresh oregano
coarse sea salt crystals

PREHEAT GRILL OR BROILER
Blend pesto with the tomatoes, salt and pepper. Brush the bread with olive oil and grill it until toasted. Immediately rub the bread with the garlic cloves which will grate into it. Smear bread with the tomato pesto, sprinkle the cheese evenly and top with the oregano and olives. Replace to the broiler to heat well and sprinkle with the sea salt before serving.

Mexican Corn Chowder

Often the most satisfying meals are those like this chowder which are served in a large bowl with a variety of side dishes, accompaniments and condiments. It has the sweet texture of corn and the deep warmth of rich Poblano chiles. The flavor is unmistakably Mexican. Serve it with some quesadillas, fresh Salsa and a simple green salad.

FOR SIX - EIGHT SERVINGS

4 *cups russet potatoes, peeled and diced into 1 inch cubes*
1 *cup diced yellow onion*
4 *seeded, diced poblanos*
2 *cups fresh corn kernels, [substitute frozen cut corn]*
3 *tablespoons minced garlic*
2 *tablespoons Canola oil*
2 *quarts milk*
⅓ *cup chopped cilantro*
1 *teaspoon oregano*
2 *teaspoons cumin*
pinch cinnamon
pinch ground cloves
1 *tablespoon sea salt*

In a sturdy soup pot heat oil. Add the vegetables and garlic. Stir while cooking until onions soften. Season with herbs, spices and salt.

Add the milk and simmer for 45 minutes, stirring occasionally. The potatoes should be very soft.

FINISHING THE SOUP

Puree the chowder in a blender or a food processor.

Serve the chowder in warmed bowls with a sprinkle of some gremolata as garnish. For added richness, top with a small dollop of room temperature sour cream.

FOR THE GREMOLATA

½ *cup fresh corn, blanched for 30 seconds*
3 *tablespoons chopped cilantro*
¼ *cup red pepper brunoise*
1 *tablespoon minced garlic*
grated zest of 1 lime

Focaccia Genovese

One of my first memories of spending time in the kitchen was being with my grandmother, Yole Magnani. She lived with my family for a couple of years when she first came to the U.S. It wasn't long before her adopted American diet needed a culinary transfusion.

When she was younger she operated a pensione in Rapallo, Italy, on the Riviera, where she prepared meals for her guests. I helped her create many of her Genovese specialties in her new American home.

One of her most treasured was Focaccia. Similar to pizza, I took an immediate liking to it. Yole was stern in her choice of only the finest olive oil, ripe plum tomatoes and capers.

Remember that working with this dough isn't difficult if you allow enough time to let the yeast work its magic. Focaccia dough is soft so it will want to stick to everything. Keep your fingers lightly floured as well as the board. If it sticks at all, scrape it off the board and redust. Be patient; eventually the dough becomes smooth and elastic. It is very important to keep the focaccia dough warm at all times.

FOR THE DOUGH

½ envelope dry yeast [1 TB]
½ cup warm water [85°]
1 tablespoon sugar
⅓ cup unbleached flour

¾ cup warm water
2¾ cup unbleached flour
1½ teaspoons kosher salt
2 tablespoons olive oil

EQUIPMENT NEEDED

9"x 13"x 1" baking sheet

Create a warm place for the dough to rise by briefly heating the oven and turning it off. Add the warm water to a warm bowl and sprinkle on the yeast. Add the sugar and the flour and blend well. Cover the bowl and place in the warm oven to rise for 10 minutes.
Add the water, salt, oil and flour. Mix well to form a soft dough.

Turn the dough onto a lightly floured board. Knead gently at first to make a smooth dough. Add ONLY enough flour to keep it from sticking. As the dough becomes elastic begin to lift it and slap it on the board briskly. Repeat 10 times. Form a ball and rub it with olive oil before placing it in a clean bowl. Cover and put it in the warmed oven to rise. It will double in about 45 minutes. Deflate the dough and replace to rise again to double.

When doubled place on an oiled baking sheet. Press out the dough with your fingertips to evenly cover the pan. It helps to do this in two stages allowing 5 minutes rest between, to let the dough relax. Leave the focaccia covered with finger indentations.

FOCACCIA TOPPING

PREHEAT OVEN TO 350°

3 tablespoons olive oil

28 ounce can of plum tomatoes, drained and squeezed

4 tablespoons capers

2 ounces grated parmigiano, romano or mozzarella

1 teaspoon coarse sea salt

Drizzle the dough with olive oil. Then spread the tomatoes, cheese and capers. Sprinkle with salt and replace to a warm place to rise. The final rise should take 10 minutes. When you notice bubbling and puffiness it is ready for the oven.

Bake focaccia for 20 - 30 minutes. The top should only brown lightly. The bread is done when it resists gentle finger pressure. Serve while still warm or at room temperature, never chilled.

OTHER POSSIBILITIES

Try adding 2 tablespoons fresh or 1 tablespoon dried herbs to the dough when it is being made. Focaccia is very often topped with only olive oil and salt, then served as a dinner bread. Other toppings for focaccia might include:

herbs: basil, rosemary, oregano

smoked cheese

sweet onions

roasted garlic

thin sliced eggplant

olives

grilled mushrooms

pesto

anchovies

pinenuts

sundried tomatoes

roasted red peppers

Sopa de Lima

The first time I enjoyed this light and refreshing soup I knew the memory would last a long time. Before the onslaught of tourism, Mexico's Cozumel was still vibrant with heady local flavors. After siesta the sleepy, narrow streets and alleys of San Miguel clattered with the sound of metal storefronts being rolled up. The pungent aromas of open kitchens emptied into the streets.

The tiny restaurant, El Foco, was animated by the rhythms of chopping and verbal banter. Thick smoke from the charcoal grill nearly cleared the room-- the vent pipe just two feet short of the ceiling. Everything on the menu was rich and authentic Yucatan.

Rustic clay bowls of salsas were present on all the small tables. The chunky salsa fresca disappeared like gaspacho while the hotter varieties rode shotgun, their fiery personalities requiring caution before approaching...and of course cerveza.

INGREDIENTS FOR 8 SERVINGS

3 pounds chicken, whole or
  pieces
1 cup diced white onion
2 diced poblanos peppers
1 cup diced carrot
2 tablespoons minced garlic
3 tablespoons chopped cilantro
2 tablespoons canola oil

2 quarts chicken stock [above]
2 cups seeded and chopped
  plum tomatoes or 1 cup
  canned diced tomatoes
1 teaspoon Mexican oregano
1 teaspoon cumin
1 tablespoon Kosher salt

Cover the chicken with the cold water. Add the salt and bring to a very gentle simmer. Cook uncovered for 2 hours. Remove the chicken to drain and cool. Remove all meat. Discard skin, bones and cartilage. Tear the meat into small pieces. Reserve. Strain the stock. Chill several hours until fat on the surface hardens. Discard the fat before using the stock.

Heat oil in heavy pot over medium heat. Add peppers, onions, garlic, carrots and cilantro. Cook for 10 minutes until the onions soften, but don't brown. Add the stock, tomatoes, cumin, oregano and salt. Simmer for 45 minutes.

2 cups diced zucchini
⅔ cup lime juice
grated zest of 1 lime
cooked chicken meat [above]

4 corn tortillas
canola oil

8 thin lime slices
sprigs of cilantro

Add the zucchini, lime juice, zest and chicken. Simmer for 20 minutes. Skim the surface to remove excess fat. The soup is ready when the squash is tender. Taste again for salt.

Cut the tortillas in half, then the halves into strips, ¼ inch wide. In a medium pan, cast iron works well, add canola oil to ½ inch depth. Heat the oil until a tortilla dropped into it sizzles immediately. Cook the strips in batches just until crisp, but not browned. Drain on paper towels. Place the chips in shallow soup bowls and ladle soup over them. Garnish with cilantro sprig and lime slice. Serve immediately.

Salsa Fresca

This is the basic raw tomato salsa served at South of the Border restaurants. Add optional heat with chopped Jalapeños or Serranos.

MAKES TWO CUPS

1⅓ cups seeded, diced ripe
   plum tomatoes
½ cup diced white onion
¼ cup cilantro,
¼ cup lime juice
2 tablespoons white vinegar
3 tablespoons finely diced
   Jalapeño or Serrano chiles
1 teaspoon sea salt

Mix all the ingredients. Let stand at least 30 minutes to marry flavors. Serve at room temperature.

Personalize Your Salsa

This recipe can be adjusted according to your tastes. If you like cilantro, add more. If you want more kick, add more chiles. Salsas are not an exact science. They should be customized exactly to your liking.

Salsa Calypso

A Yucatan classic packing both the serious heat and the perfume of the bold chile Serrano. Definitely NOT for the faint of tongue.

MAKES ONE CUP

½ cup diced white onions
½ cup chopped chile Serranos
½ cup lime juice
4 tablespoons chopped cilantro
1 teaspoon sea salt

Mix all the ingredients. Marinate 30 minutes before serving.

Salsa Ranchera

A dark, rich salsa - great with grilled meats, fish, eggs or frijoles.

MAKES TWO CUPS

10 plum tomatoes
2 small onions, peeled & halved
4 garlic cloves
2 tablespoons canola oil
1 canned chipotle chile in adobo
1 tablespoon brown sugar
1 teaspoon oregano
2 tablespoons lime juice
2 teaspoons kosher salt

PREHEAT CHARCOAL GRILL

Put the tomatoes and onions on a very hot grill. Let them cook until evenly charred. Set aside.
Over medium heat cook the garlic in the canola oil until golden. Add the tomatoes, onions and the rest of the ingredients. Cook at gentle simmer for 30 minutes. Add a little water if it becomes too dry. Puree the mixture until smooth. Taste for salt and adjust if necessary. Serve at room temperature.

Quesadillas Mexicanas

In Mexico quesadillas are made exclusively with corn tortillas. We have adapted them to flour tortillas. Try this traditional version for a change with Salsa Verde for the taste of old Mexico.

MAKES 8 QUESADILLAS

8 fresh corn tortillas
10 ounces queso Asadero, or
    monterey jack
½ cup canola oil

PREHEAT SMALL CAST IRON SKILLET

Heat oil in hot skillet and fry the corn tortilla for 15 seconds, not crisp. Put some cheese in the center and fold the tortilla. Cook 30 seconds more on each side to melt the cheese and serve.

Salsa Verde

This is a cooked salsa which is served at room temperature. It features the tomatillo, which resembles a small green tomato with a dry, papery husk...very Mexican.

MAKES TWO CUPS

2 cups husked and quartered
  tomatillos
1 tablespoon canola oil
⅔ cup diced white onion
4 whole garlic cloves
⅔ cup chopped cilantro
¼ cup water
¼ cup white vinegar
2 tablespoons sugar
2 teaspoons kosher salt
1 teaspoon oregano
4 arbol chiles [optional]

Cook the onions and garlic in the oil until soft. Add the other ingredients and simmer for 30 minutes. Remove the arbol chiles. Puree, then cool the salsa and serve at room temperature.

Caesar Salad

This very popular salad has been around for a long time. As its popularity has increased so has the number of versions and variations. It began as a table-side preparation done by a waiter as an up-scale show and has progressed to the salad bar at Wendy's. How's that for mainstream!

The classic Caesar included raw egg in the dressing, however with our new awareness of Salmonella bacteria, preparations have been altered to either eliminate the egg altogether or include it in a safer form. This recipe uses commercial mayonnaise as the base so it stores perfectly in the refrigerator.

Romaine is the traditional choice of lettuce because it's crispiness is a good balance for the richness of the dressing. Hearts of romaine are ideal if you can find them.

FOR 8 SERVINGS

INGREDIENTS FOR CROUTONS

2 cups French bread, cut into
   ¾ inch cubes
⅓ cup olive oil
1 teaspoon kosher salt
½ teaspoon pepper

PREHEAT OVEN TO 350°
EQUIPMENT NEEDED
Large baking sheet

Place bread cubes into a bowl and toss with the olive oil, salt and pepper. Spread out on a baking sheet. Bake for about 15 minutes, stirring often, until they are evenly toasted. Remove, cool and store in an airtight container.

FOR THE CAESAR DRESSING
MAKES 1 ½ CUPS

½ cup mayonnaise
1½ teaspoons minced garlic
2 tablespoons fresh lemon juice
2 tablespoons red wine vinegar
3 teaspoons Dijon mustard
4 teaspoons [1oz] crushed
   anchovy filets
1 tablespoon anchovy oil [above]
2 tablespoons grated
   Parmigiano-Reggiano
⅔ cup olive oil
½ teaspoon kosher salt
½ teaspoon black pepper

Crush the anchovies with the back of a spoon. Add them to the mayonnaise with the garlic, mustard and cheese. Stir in the lemon juice and the vinegar. With a whisk, or in a food processor, slowly add the oils while beating. Season with salt and pepper. Refrigerate for 1 hour to let the flavors marry.

ASSEMBLING THE SALAD

2 heads torn Romaine lettuce*
½ cup shaved parmigiano
croutons
Caesar dressing

The salad can be dressed up to 10 minutes prior to serving, but it is best served immediately. Toss the lettuce and croutons with the dressing to coat evenly. Serve on chilled plates or on a platter for buffet service. Garnish with the shaved parmigiano.

*Note- If using hearts, the leaves may be left whole for an attractive presentation.

Santa Fe Cabbage and Jicama Slaw

This is a refreshing detour from classic summer slaw. The character of this slaw is warmly enhanced by the fresh roasted, ground chiles. Chile powders range in taste from mild to very fiery. Their heat mostly depends on the pepper variety and seed content. Freshly ground chiles have the best flavor. Old mixtures are often bitter or flat in taste. Don't use a chile and cumin blend-- add cumin to your own taste.

FOR EIGHT SERVINGS

5 cups finely sliced cabbage
2 cups julienned jicama
1 cup diced red onion
1 cup diced red pepper
⅓ cup chopped cilantro

Toss the cabbage, jicama, peppers, onions and cilantro in a large bowl.

¾ cup salad oil
1 tablespoon minced garlic
¼ cup red vinegar
¼ cup lime juice
¼ cup fresh orange juice
¼ cup dark ground chiles
1 teaspoon Mexican oregano
2 tablespoons brown sugar
1 teaspoon ground cumin
⅛ teaspoon cayenne pepper
1½ teaspoons sea salt

Mix all other ingredients in separate bowl. Pour this over the salad mixture and toss to coat evenly.

Grilled Shrimp Salad with Black Beans and Corn

A colorful variety of flavors and textures makes this hearty salad a summer luncheon main dish, served with garlic baked tortilla points and fresh tomatillo salsa on page 14.

INGREDIENTS FOR 8 SERVINGS

2 pounds medium shrimp, peeled and deveined

Remove shells and tails from the shrimp. Make a shallow cut along the back and remove the 'vein'. Rinse and drain the shrimp, then dry them on paper towel.

FOR SHRIMP MARINADE

3 tablespoons salad oil
3 tablespoons lime juice
1 grated lime zest
2 tablespoons minced garlic
2 tablespoons orange juice
  concentrate
3 tablespoons chopped cilantro
½ teaspoon oregano
1 teaspoon ground cumin
½ teaspoon kosher salt
pinch cinnamon
pinch ground anise seed

Place ingredients for the marinade in a food processor. Pulse to quickly blend. Add to the shrimp, toss to coat and refrigerate for 2 hours. The shrimp are best cooked on a charcoal grill. Cook them for one minute on each side, or until opaque, then refrigerate.

INGREDIENTS FOR DRESSING

½ cup salad oil
¼ cup lime juice
½ cup orange juice
2 tablespoons cider vinegar
1 tablespoon minced garlic
1 teaspoon cumin
2 teaspoons oregano
2 tablespoons brown sugar
1 teaspoon sea salt

6 cups cooked black beans,
  rinsed and drained
2 cups fresh cut corn
1 cup diced red pepper
1 poblano pepper, roasted,
  peeled and diced, page 102
1 cup chopped green onion
¼ cup chopped cilantro

Blend all the ingredients for the dressing. Stir well to dissolve the brown sugar.

Gently mix the black beans, corn, peppers, chopped green onions and cilantro. Add the dressing and toss again, just to coat.

Lightly oil the green onions and grill them, turning once. Set aside.

Place the salad on a shallow platter and arrange the grilled shrimp on top. Garnish with the grilled green onions and lime wedges.

FOR GARNISH

12 green onions, grilled

Oriental Noodle Salad

This simple pasta salad is best made at least a day in advance. It can easily be transformed into a light main dish with the addition of steamed vegetables, cooked chilled seafood or grilled chicken.

FOR 6 - 8 SERVINGS

1 pound Spaghettini or Linguine, DeCecco or equivalent quality

Cook the pasta in salted boiling water until al dente. Drain, refresh and hold.

FOR THE DRESSING

¼ cup toasted sesame seed oil
⅔ cup salad oil
½ cup dark soy sauce
¼ cup hoisin sauce
3 tablespoons rice vinegar
¼ cup black sesame seeds
⅓ cup diced red pepper
1 cup chopped green onions

Mix the dressing in a bowl. Add it to the pasta. Mix and set aside for at least 12 hours. Toss with the green onions and peppers before serving.

POSSIBLE ADDITIONS MIGHT INCLUDE

1 cup green peas
1 cup julienned carrots, blanched 1 minute
1 cup snow peas, blanched 1 minute and refreshed

2 cups cut broccoli florettes, blanched and refreshed
1 cup cooked shrimp, squid, sea scallops or crabmeat
1 cup pulled chicken meat

Balsamic Vinaigrette

MAKES TWO CUPS

2 tablespoons minced shallots
1 teaspoon minced garlic
1 tablespoon Dijon mustard
⅓ cup red wine vinegar
⅓ cup Balsamic vinegar
1 cup canola oil
⅓ cup olive oil
1 teaspoon kosher salt
¼ teaspoon black pepper
1 teaspoon sugar

Put all the ingredients except the oils in the bowl of a food processor and blend. With the blade spinning, add the oils slowly to blend.

Curried Chicken Salad

SERVES SIX-EIGHT

1 three pound chicken, boiled,
   cooled and picked
3 cups peeled, diced crisp apple
1 cup diced scallions
1 cup diced sweet red pepper
1 cup green peas
1 tablespoon kosher salt
1 teaspoon Tabasco sauce
½ cup toasted coconut flakes
⅔ cup raisins
1 cup mayonnaise
1 cup nonfat plain yogurt
⅓ cup honey
4 tablespoons fresh curry powder
[the amount will vary depending
on the strength]

The chicken should be left in small chunks, free of skin and bones. Mix all the ingredients in a bowl. Remember not all curry powders are the same, so adjust the amount according to your taste.

Note: In this salad the mayonnaise can be replaced by yogurt or lowfat sour cream, but reduce the *total* to 1½ cups.

Garlic Baked Tortilla Points

EQUIPMENT NEEDED
Large baking sheet

1 dozen seven inch flour
   tortillas
½ cup salad or canola oil
3 tablespoons minced garlic

2 tablespoons paprika
2 tablespoons chile powder
1 teaspoon cumin
⅛ teaspoon cayenne
2 teaspoons sea salt

PREHEAT OVEN TO 325°

Cook the garlic in the oil over low heat for 5 minutes. Don't brown it. Cut the stacked tortillas into eight wedges each. Brush them with the garlic oil. Place the tortillas on the baking sheet in one layer and bake until crispy. Continue to finish all the tortillas.

Blend the seasonings with the salt and toss the tortillas to lightly coat them.

Sesame Tempura Squid On Spinach and Napa Cabbage

This is a very popular salad at our poolside lunches and it is substantial enough to be served as a principal dish. The crunchy coated squid are joined with greens that together are dressed with a sweet and sour dressing called 'Hong Kong Sunset'.

SERVES SIX TO EIGHT

PREPARING THE SQUID

2 *pounds fresh cleaned squid*
1 *cup whole milk*

Cut the squid tubes into ½ inch wide rings. Hold in the milk for 4 hours prior to cooking.

FOR THE SALAD

3 *cups sliced napa cabbage*
6 *cups torn spinach leaves*
2 *cups julienned jicama*
1 *cup chopped scallions*
6 *ounces enoki mushrooms*
½ *cup finely diced red pepper*
cilantro sprigs [optional]

Gently toss salad ingredients in a bowl.
Mix dry ingredients for the batter. Slowly add the club soda while stirring. Beat until smooth with a whisk and let stand in the freezer for 10 minutes to chill well.

FOR THE FRYING BATTER

2 *cups unbleached flour*
⅓ *cup potato starch*
1 *teaspoon baking powder*
1 *teaspoon kosher salt*
⅓ *cup sesame seeds*
2 *cups club soda*
¼ *cup shoyu*

Pot for deep-frying
2 *quarts canola oil*

Heat the frying oil to 350°.
Drain the squid and batter it lightly. Fry it for 30 seconds and drain it on paper towels. Cook it in small batches so the oil temperature doesn't drop during cooking. Hold the cooked squid warm.
Toss the salad with ⅔ cup dressing and place it on a serving platter. Arrange the fried squid on the greens and drizzle with remaining dressing.

1 *cup Hong Kong Sunset*
   Dressing, page 24
1 *cup chopped scallions*
½ *cup cilantro leaves [optional]*
2 *tablespoons black sesame seeds*

Garnish with cilantro or chopped scallions and sesame seeds.

Grilled Zucchini with Warm Tomato Vinaigrette

We created this salad specially for zucchini squash but quickly found it was equally delicious with yellow summer squash, eggplant and even asparagus...or a mix of all of them.

INGREDIENTS FOR 8 SERVINGS

6 medium zucchini squash
⅔ cup olive oil
2 tablespoons kosher salt

FOR THE VINAIGRETTE

3 cups peeled, seeded and diced
    ripe plum tomatoes
3 tablespoons minced shallots
1 tablespoon minced garlic
⅓ cup chopped parsley
¼ cup chopped chervil [optional]
⅔ cup olive oil
⅓ cup balsamic vinegar
2 tablespoons dijon mustard
3 tablespoons honey
1 teaspoon crushed fennel
    seeds*
3 tablespoons capers
½ teaspoon black pepper
2 teaspoons sea salt

SPECIAL EQUIPMENT NEEDED

Charcoal, gas or electric broiler

Trim the ends from the zucchini. Slice them lengthwise into slices ⅛ inch thick. Brush both sides *lightly* with olive oil, salt and cook on a hot grill. Set aside.

Heat 1 tablespoon of the olive oil in a saucepan. Add the shallots and garlic. Cook until soft. Add tomatoes, parsley, chervil, fennel seed, salt and pepper. Simmer for 15 minutes. Add the remaining olive oil, vinegar, honey, mustard and capers. Simmer for 10 minutes.

Arrange the zucchini on a platter. Stir the vinaigrette well. Ladle the sauce over the squash and serve.

*Note--An electric spice mill or a coffee grinder works well, or fennel seeds can be crushed between a heavy skillet and a thick cutting board.

Baby Tomato Salad with Croutons

The inspiration for this summer salad came with the arrival of a new crop of bright red, organically grown cherry tomatoes called Sweet 100's. Moments after coming off the truck we were popping these sweet, juicy gems into our mouths and sharing blissful grins. Try to locate fully ripe tomatoes, or grow them yourself. Sun-ripened tomatoes can't compare with the hard, tasteless grocery store variety.

INGREDIENTS FOR 8 SERVINGS

4 cups baby tomatoes

FOR THE CROUTONS

4 cups cubed French bread
⅓ cup olive oil
½ teaspoon oregano
½ teaspoon basil
½ teaspoon rosemary
½ teaspoon crushed fennel seed
2 tablespoons minced garlic
½ teaspoon black pepper
2 teaspoons coarse sea salt
3 tablespoons grated Romano
½ cup Champagne vinaigrette,
  [recipe follows]

PREHEAT OVEN TO 325°

Combine the herbs, garlic and olive oil in a bowl. Add the bread and toss with the herb mixture to evenly mix. Spread the cubes onto a baking sheet. Sprinkle them with salt and pepper. Bake for fifteen minutes, stirring them often. They are done when golden brown. Sprinkle with cheese and let them cool on the pan. Toss the tomatoes, croutons and vinaigrette to coat evenly. Serve at room temperature.

Champagne Vinaigrette

MAKES ONE CUP

4 tablespoons minced shallots
1 tablespoon minced garlic
1 tablespoon Dijon mustard
1 teaspoon sea salt
1 tablespoon sugar
⅓ cup Champagne vinegar
⅔ cup salad oil
½ teaspoon white pepper

Blend all the ingredients except the oil in a food processor. Slowly add the oil while spinning until it is fully incorporated.

Hummous

I often hear comments from our guests about our surprising selection of dishes offered at a guest ranch. I enjoy this kind of input because it means that our guests are open to the wide variety that we as cooks also enjoy. This Middle-Eastern favorite always gets raves from its many fans. Garbanzo beans are an easy legume to cook, and many acceptable canned products are available. Hummous is a good source of protein and can be made in many variations.

INGREDIENTS FOR 8 SERVINGS

3 cups cooked garbanzo beans
   with cooking liquid or two
   15 ounce cans
⅓ cup cooking juice or liquid
3 tablespoons toasted tahini
⅓ cup olive oil
3 tablespoons lemon juice
2 teaspoons chopped garlic
1½ teaspoons cumin
⅛ teaspoon cayenne pepper
¾ teaspoon sea salt
4 tablespoons chopped parsley

In a food processor add all the ingredients. Puree till smooth.

To create a slightly different version, try adding:
roasted garlic, curry powder, roasted red peppers or saffron

Lentil - Walnut Paté

This is a highly nutritious vegetarian spread that couldn't be further from a true paté. It is served as a dip, and it is great as a slather on sandwiches. Try it with the herbed roasted pita chips, page 24.

MAKES THREE CUPS

2 cups cooked lentils, [page 59]
1 cup walnuts
⅓ cup Shoyu or Tamari
¼ cup chopped parsley
3 tablespoons minced shallots
2 tablespoons minced garlic
⅛ teaspoon cayenne

In a food processor puree the lentils, walnuts, shallots, garlic, parsley and shoyu until smooth. Add a little lentil cooking water as needed for consistency. The mixture should be smooth and creamy.

Roasted Herbed Pita Chips

This is an easy to prepare all purpose chip that is great for dipping, to serve with cheese or eaten by themselves. Make plenty because they vanish quickly. Store leftovers in an airtight container.

MAKES FOUR DOZEN   PREHEAT OVEN TO 325°

3 tablespoons minced garlic
½ cup olive oil
6 loaves pita bread
3 tablespoons herbs de Provence*
2 teaspoons coarse sea salt
½ teaspoon black pepper
* Herbs de Provence is a
French blend of rosemary,
thyme, basil, savory, marjoram, fennel and lavender.

Cook the garlic in the olive oil until soft, then set it aside to cool. Brush the pitas with the garlic oil. Cut each loaf into 8 wedges. Place them on a baking sheet and season with the herbs, salt and pepper. Bake until toasted, approximately 20 minutes. Turn them while they cook to roast evenly. They can be served warm or when cool.

Hong Kong Sunset Dressing

The ranch cooks created this dressing by collaboration when we needed a dressing for a spinach salad. We wanted something sweet and sour, a good combination with spinach. We gathered some Chinese ingredients and away we went. Then we needed to name it. I had recently received a letter from a friend, Johnny Roos, who was cooking in Hong Kong. In it he colorfully described the city and a late day harbor scene...and we had *our* very own Hong Kong Sunset.

MAKES 3 CUPS

2 tablespoons minced ginger
2 tablespoons minced garlic
peeled zest from ¼ orange
⅔ cup rice vinegar
⅔ cup shoyu
¼ cup honey
½ cup ketchup
⅓ cup sesame oil
⅓ cup canola oil
¼ teaspoon cayenne

Put all the ingredients except the oils in a food processor or blender. Puree until smooth. With the blade spinning slowly pour the oils into the mixture.

This dressing keeps well when refrigerated for up to two weeks.

Marinated Salmon Salad

I was introduced to this salad during a stay with some friends who live in London. In the comfortable and warm home of artists and antique experts Robert and Josyane Young, a most memorable meal was presented with the inimitable ease and grace reserved for natural cooks of the highest metier. The elegance of this recipe is surpassed only by its simplicity. The salmon is 'cooked' by the citrus resembling lox in texture. Choose a fine wine vinegar to add the needed component of tart fruitiness.

INGREDIENTS FOR 8 SERVINGS

1 pound salmon, boneless and skinless

¼ cup lemon juice

¼ cup Champagne vinegar

2 teaspoons sugar

2 teaspoons Dijon mustard

1 teaspoon kosher salt

¼ teaspoon white pepper

2 heads romaine lettuce

½ cup salad oil

3 tablespoons minced shallots

¼ cup chopped parsley

½ teaspoon black pepper

Slice the salmon into paper-thin slices ½ inch wide, approximately two inches long.

Mix the lemon juice, vinegar, sugar, mustard, salt and pepper. Add the salmon and toss well. Marinate it for 30 minutes refrigerated.

Wash the romaine, drain and dry it thoroughly. Tear the lettuce into pieces and hold it in a serving bowl.

Add the oil, shallots and parsley to the salmon and its marinade. Mix it well then toss it with the romaine. Serve with fresh black pepper.

Warm Goat Cheese Salad

During a recent stay in France we found this salad on nearly every menu in one regional form or another. They use the log shaped, soft ripened goat cheese known as Bucheron, which when sliced fits nicely on the slice of baguette. For this salad I like to use a blend of baby lettuces and greens, known as Mesclun mix. Another choice is Boston or bib lettuce which closely resembles French 'laitue'.

FOR 8 SERVINGS

16 slices baguette, ½ inch thick
16 slices Bucheron, ¼ inch thick
whole garlic cloves

FOR THE DRESSING

¼ cup champagne vinegar
⅓ cup salad oil
1 tablespoon minced shallots
1 teaspoon dijon mustard
½ teaspoon minced garlic
1 teaspoon sugar
½ teaspoon kosher salt
¼ teaspoon white pepper

1 pound assorted baby greens
   or torn Boston lettuce

PREHEAT BROILER

Place the slices of bread on a baking sheet. Place under broiler to toast lightly. Turn over and repeat. Rub the bread with garlic and top with a slice of cheese.

Blend the dressing in a large bowl. Just prior to serving toss the lettuce with the dressing. Place toasts with cheese into the broiler until it begins to melt.

Serve the dressed salad on plates with two cheese toasts on each.

Honey Mustard Horseradish Vinaigrette

MAKES ONE PINT

½ cup red wine vinegar
2 tablespoons whole grain
   Dijon mustard
4 tablespoons honey
3 tablespoons horseradish
1 teaspoon minced garlic
1 teaspoon basil
½ teaspoon oregano
1 teaspoon thyme
3 tablespoons minced shallot
¼ cup olive oil
¾ cup salad oil
1 teaspoon kosher salt
¾ teaspoon black pepper

Place all the ingredients except the oils in a food processor. Pulse to blend.

While processor blade is spinning slowly pour the oils into the bowl to blend thoroughly.

Let stand for at least one hour to allow the dried herbs to rehydrate.

CHAPTER TWO

Fish and Seafood

Wyoming is great beef country and our guests often enjoy the hearty menus to sustain them through a hard day's activities. I depend heavily on fish and seafoods to provide a balance for the heavier ranch fare. Many of our guests are incredulous to find fresh fish in the 'middle of nowhere'. Because we utilize very dependable transportation services, we are able to offer the freshest fish available anywhere.

We take great pride in serving a wide variety of seafoods from around the world. Our purveyors have earned our trust just as yours should. Your requirements when shopping for fish should be the same as ours. Visit the market first to discuss your needs and from an informed position ask plenty of questions. Find out when they receive the fish you want and buy it that same day.

Fresh fish is best prepared soon after buying it but there are ways to store it properly if necessary. Whole fish keep better than filets or cut fish, since the meat hasn't been exposed to warm air, hands and organisms responsible for deterioration. Whole fish can be packed in ice, protected by its skin and abdominal membrane. Cut fish should be protected from direct contact with ice as it tends to leach out juices and color. Wrap fileted fish loosely in waxed paper or freezer paper and store in the coldest part of your refrigerator.

Only under the rarest circumstances could I recommend preparing frozen fish. After fish has been frozen, too many essential fluids leave the flesh during thawing. The texture is changed and no matter how much care is taken to cook it, the fish will always have a stronger flavor and drier taste. Use great care while cooking previously frozen fish. Remember it cooks much faster than fresh fish since it contains less water. Don't overcook it, and always serve immediately-- it will become tough and dry if left to stand even 5 minutes. Of course some fresh products are difficult to obtain. Shrimp is a good example. You may find fresh rock shrimp to buy instead of frozen white shrimp for applications when size isn't important, like in gumbo, stews or pasta sauces. Rock shrimp are much smaller, but they remain tender and succulent.

Whenever possible ask your fish market to filet, bone or skin your purchase. Unless you have the skill and equipment it makes sense to start with a recipe-ready product. In the event you may need the scraps for stock, they will gladly wrap them up for you to take home.

This discussion wouldn't be complete without mentioning the safety of our oceans' bounty as it pertains to our diet. Overfishing, pollution and crowded farming techniques can risk the quality of our food. Take great care in choosing your seafood provider for you are trusting them with great responsibility, especially in terms of shellfish, where more potential exists for tainted products. The U.S. Department of Commerce inspects our seafood, but *your* knowledge is the best test. Expect to pay top dollar for quality at a market with a good reputation.

Choose wild seafoods whenever possible and try the quality aquaculture items available: tilapia, red trout, catfish, salmon and mussels. Keep in mind that farmed salmon is artificially colored. Wild salmon is available during the late spring and summer months and in my opinion is superior to the farmed products. Certain fish are more prone to tumors and flukes. These include swordfish, halibut and amberjack. Inspect the meat carefully before you take it home. Warm water fish have a shorter shelf life than those from colder ocean waters.

A general guide when preparing fish is to figure about 10 minutes cooking per inch of thickness, measured at the thickest part. Fish is cooked when under gentle pressure the meat flakes or breaks. All fish does not cook the same so look for clues like a change in color from transluscent to opaque. Try to keep fish moist and tender by not overcooking it. Remember that fish holding in hot cooking liquid will continue to cook even when off the heat.

Our oceans' bounty is a great resource when managed well and not taken for granted. We need to remain vigilant of the issues of pollution and overfishing if this great food source is to be available to generations to come.

Halibut With Chive Butter Sauce

This is a quick and easy preparation that uses a minimum of butter in the sauce. The ingenious component helping to enrich the sauce is potato cooking water. The accompaniment of boiled baby creamers provides this necessary ingredient.

FOR SIX SERVINGS

PREPARING THE POTATOES

1½ *pounds new potatoes*

1 *teaspoon kosher salt*

Carefully peel the potatoes and trim into barrel shapes. Cut them in half lengthwise. Barely cover with salted water and simmer until tender. Drain and reserve the water for the fish sauce.

EQUIPMENT NEEDED

A heavy ovenproof pan just large enough to hold the fish

PREHEAT OVEN TO 400°

6 *six ounce filets of halibut, cod, haddock, sole or seabass*

1½ *cup fish stock [see page 30]*

½ *cup potato water*

3 *tablespoons chopped chives*

pinch salt

pinch white pepper

Place the fish in the pan, skinned side down. Add the stock and potato water. Season with salt and pepper. Add the chives. Bring quickly to a simmer, cover loosely with foil and steam the filets for about 10 minutes. The fish will look opaque and it will flake under gentle pressure when done. Hold the fish warm while making the sauce.

FOR THE SAUCE

6 *tablespoons soft butter,*

2 *tablespoons chopped chives*

12 *whole chives*

Place the fish pan on high heat and bring the cooking liquid to a fast boil. When reduced to 1 cup add the butter. Boil the sauce vigorously for about 30 seconds until it is thick and foamy. Once the sauce is made check that the fish is hot. Reheat briefly if necessary. Spoon sauce over the fish. Sprinkle with chives. Garnish with whole chives.

Fish Stock

Fish stock is as important to the flavoring of fish and seafood dishes as meat stock is to sauces and meat preparations. It is made from the bones and scraps of fish that are low in oil. Fish that are high in oil tend to develop unpleasantly strong flavors when cooked for stock. The best fish to use in making stock are cold water varieties, or the so-called 'noble fish', from the French description: sole, turbot, plaice, halibut and the cods.

MAKES ONE QUART

1 pound fish bones
5 cups water
1 cup dry white wine
4 inch bouquet garni
8 black peppercorns

Gently simmer the bones in the water with the bouquet garni, white wine and peppercorns. Skim the surface to remove impurities and oils that rise as scum. Cook for 30 minutes and strain.

Choosing Wine For Cooking Fish and Seafood

Contrary to general practice, wine used in all cooking, including fish, should always be of very good quality. It needs to be able to stand up to the high heat of cooking which can make a poor wine taste even worse. Remember too that any distinctive flavors will be intensified so choose the wine carefully. Always use dry varieties including Sauvignon Blanc, Pinot Blanc and lighter Chardonnays. Often the rich Chardonnays are too fruity or oaky to pair well with the delicate flavors of certain seafood preparations. It is recommended to drink the same wine used in cooking a dish.

Serving White Wines

Less wine buckets are being used at the tables of fine restaurants. We are learning to appreciate a wine's qualities when tasted at cellar temperatures. Gone are the days when all white wine was automatically served icy cold. At these temperatures the flavors are hidden and untastable. Winemakers are producing smooth and fragrant examples of all white wine varieties and they want us to **taste** their results. So pass on the icy bath and enjoy these wines at around 58°-62°.

Rocky Mountain Trout

Opportunity abounds at the A Bar A to challenge your flyfishing skills within the sporting waters of the ranch's streams and river. The North Platte, with its wide dominance, requires different techniques than its neighboring tributaries, Big Creek, Mullen Creek and Savage Creek. Often the delicious reward is proudly served for breakfast or dinner among envious friends in our convivial dining room.

The A Bar A fish are so fresh, only a minimum of preparation preserves the delicacy of our Rocky Mountain trout. Allow one 8 -10 oz. cleaned and boned fish per person. Rinse the fish under cold water and dry the it with paper towels inside and out. Preparation can include removing the head if desired, and the fins can also be cut off with scissors. Your fish market can do this for you. This recipe is our traditional Ranch breakfast preparation.

EQUIPMENT NEEDED
Heavy ovenproof saute pan
large enough for the fish

INGREDIENTS FOR 4 FISH
4 eight ounce boned trout
2 large beaten eggs
2 tablespoons water
¼ teaspoon kosher salt
¼ teaspoon white pepper
1 cup bacon fat or salad oil
1 cup stone ground organic
  yellow cornmeal
½ teaspoon kosher salt
pinch pepper
lemon wedges

PREHEAT OVEN TO 400°

In a shallow dish beat eggs with water, salt and pepper. Season the cavity of the trout with salt and pepper. Coat the fish in the egg mixture and drain them. Roll the fish inthe cornmeal mixture to coat them evenly.

Heat the bacon fat over medium-high heat until nearly smoking. Carefully place fish into the pan. Cook until the underside is golden brown. Turn the fish and place the pan in the oven to finish, about 10 minutes.

The trout is done when the thickest spot of the back leaves a slight indentation when pressed with a finger. Drain on a paper towel and serve with lemon wedges.

Grilled Trout with Provençal Herbs and Vegetables

Grilling whole trout offers a lowfat and delicious alternative to pan frying. The presentation is casual and the captured aromas are memorable. When larger fish are grilled sometimes it is helpful to finish cooking them in the oven. Natural charcoal or wood chips can add even more flavor during grilling.

FOR PREPARING FOUR TROUT

4 eight ounce boned trout
½ lemon
kosher salt and pepper

12 sprigs parsley
12 large bay leaves
12 stems fresh thyme
12 stems fresh rosemary
infused olive oil [page 33]

Prep trout [see previous recipe]. Open the trout and sprinkle with a fews drops of lemon juice and a pinch of salt and pepper.

Place the parsley, thyme and rosemary on a cutting board. With the back of a heavy knife bruise the herbs with several blows, especially the stems. This will release the essential oils. Stuff each trout with equal amounts of the herbs. Return the fish to their original shape. With a knife score the skin on both sides of the fish 3 or 4 times and brush with the infused oil.

GRILLING THE TROUT

White, ashen coals indicate the fire is ready. The heat of the coals determines how near the fire the fish is cooked. An 8 - 10 ounce fish cooks about eight minutes on each side over moderate heat.

Both the fish and the grill need to be lightly oiled just before cooking. Don't use too much or it will drip into the fire and cause unpleasant flares and a sooty taste.

Some of the skin may burn during the grilling. But be careful, if the fire is too hot too much skin will burn away before the meat underneath is cooked. Raise the grill or pull the fish off and cool down the fire with some water so the fish can finish cooking evenly.

Press firmly with your finger on the back of the fish near the dorsal fin. If the indentation stays the fish is done.

FOR THE GRILLED VEGETABLES

Vidalia or any sweet onions,
sliced into ½ inch thick rounds
large asparagus
plum tomatoes

infused olive oil
kosher salt
black pepper
Balsamic or sherry vinegar

Place asparagus on a flat surface. Holding the tip remove the tough skin with a vegetable peeler starting from below the 'buds' down the shaft to the end. Trim 2 inches from the bottom end of each one. Blanch them for 5 minutes until tender. Refresh in cold water and drain. Remove the stem and halve the tomatoes, cutting from top to bottom.

Lightly oil the grill. Brush the vegetables lightly with olive oil and cook them until they are marked on both sides. Season with salt and pepper as they cook. Remember that onions cook longest, followed by the tomatoes and asparagus. Serve them warm with a splash of Balsamic or sherry vinegar.

OTHER VEGETABLES GREAT FOR GRILLING

potatoes	*eggplant*	*peppers*
squashes	*carrots*	*fennel*
corn	*cauliflower*	*mushrooms*

Infused Olive Oil

Oils infused with the tastes of herbs, peppers, garlic, citrus or truffles are very good way to season foods. Any culinary oil can be used for this purpose and olive oils add an exceptional dimension. Dried herbs used for infusions should be left on the branch whenever possible. Garlic should be roasted or blanched first. Cook the infusion over *very low* heat for 15 minutes before storing in a covered jar or a bottle. The quantity of herbs used is a matter of personal taste. Experiment to find the tastes you like best. Try these:

rosemary	*orange peel*
thyme	*dried hot peppers*
bay leaf	*peppercorns*
garlic	*fennel seed*

Pumpkinseed Roasted Ahi With Adobado and Pineapple Salsa

This dish is typical of 'convergence cuisine'-- bringing together the popular tastes and textures of the Pacific Rim and the vibrant flavors of the new Southwest. Yellowfin tuna, *Ahi* in Hawaiian, should be cooked to medium, or less, so it remains tender and juicy. Pineapple salsa adds a colorful dimension of crisp, tart sweetness that balances the chipotle pepper's smoky heat.

MAKES SIX SERVINGS

FOR THE CRUST

1 cup raw pepitas
1 teaspoon kosher salt

FOR THE ADOBADO GLAZE

8 dried chipotle chiles
3 tablespoons lime juice
2 tablespoons chopped cilantro
6 cloves roasted garlic
½ cup brown sugar
4 tablespoons canola oil
1 teaspoon kosher salt

FOR THE SALSA

In ⅛ inch dice:
¾ cup fresh pineapple
¼ cup anaheim pepper
¼ cup red onion
¼ cup red pepper

2 tablespoons chopped cilantro
1 teaspoon minced garlic
1 teaspoon minced ginger
4 tablespoons lime juice
1 teaspoon kosher salt

PREHEAT OVEN TO 350°

Grind the pepitas and salt in a food processor until it resembles coarse cornmeal.

Roast the chiles in the oven for 5 minutes. Wearing rubber gloves, remove the stems and seeds. Barely cover the chiles with water and simmer for 15 minutes until soft. Drain them. In a food processor puree the garlic, chiles, lime juice, sugar, cilantro, oil and salt until very smooth. Set aside.

Mix the diced pineapple, peppers and onion with the other ingredients. Toss to blend and refrigerate for one hour before using.

Fruit Salsas

Many fruits can be used in salsa. Instead of pineapple in the preceding recipe try pear, kiwifruit, nectarine, avocado, jicama, papaya, Asian pear...

EQUIPMENT NEEDED

OVENPROOF SKILLET JUST
LARGE ENOUGH FOR THE FISH

6 *six ounce ahi steaks, cut*
   ¾ inch thick
4 *tablespoons canola oil*
1 *teaspoon sesame oil*

Brush the tuna steaks with the glaze and dredge them in the pepita meal, pressing firmly to form a crust. Heat the oils in a heavy, ovenproof skillet just large enough for the six steaks. Cook the tuna over medium heat until golden brown. Turn the fish and put the skillet in the oven to roast the fish for about 15 minutes. The tuna should still be pink and moist. Don't overcook it. Garnish with the salsa and serve over Oriental Noodles, recipe on page 20.

Arctic Char with Shallot -Tomato Concassée and Cream

One of the recent successes of the fish farming industry is Iceland's Arctic Char. The fish is related to trout, its meat is red and like all farm-raised fish, it has a long shelf life. Serve this rich and delicate Char with rice pilaf and an elegant Viognier from Calera Winery.

SERVES SIX

6 *six ounce Char filets*
2 *tablespoons sweet butter*
⅔ *cup fish stock*
¼ *cup minced shallots*
¼ *cup chopped chervil or parsley*
1 *cup peeled, seeded and diced*
   ripe plum tomatoes
½ *teaspoon sea salt*
pinch white pepper
1 *cup heavy cream*
2 *tablespoons lemon juice*

In a heavy skillet cook shallots in butter until soft. Place the fish skin side down over the shallots. Add the fish stock, salt, pepper, tomatoes and half the chervil. Bring to a gentle simmer, then cover and steam for 5 minutes. Remove the fish to a warm platter to hold. To the skillet add the cream and lemon juice. Reduce quickly until thickened. Adjust for salt to taste. Spoon the sauce over the fish and garnish with the remaining chervil.

Seafood Gumbo

The cooking of Louisiana is a common crave. Once the Crescent City undresses itself before your eyes, you feel destined to return, and return. It may be the memory of a crazy Mardi Gras, an innocent tourist visit, or just a plain and simple romance. This love affair with honest, no-frills Cajun cookin' becomes a deep affection. No dish better represents the mysterious uncertainty or gastronomic expectations of New Orleans than rich, dark gumbo.

SERVES EIGHT

FOR THE ROUX

¼ cup canola oil

½ cup flour

2 tablespoons margarine

1 cup diced onions

1 cup diced celery

2 tablespoons minced garlic

½ cup diced green pepper

1 cup diced plum tomatoes

⅔ cup tomato puree

1½ cup cut okra

½ cup chopped parsley

2 teaspoons chopped thyme

1 tablespoon filé gumbo

2 teaspoons Cajun Spice,
   see page 41

6 bay leaves

2 teaspoons kosher salt

In a small heavy skillet, preferably cast iron, cook the flour and the oil over medium-low heat while stirring occasionally, until it is the color of milk chocolate .

In a soup pot cook the celery, onions, peppers and garlic in the margarine until soft. Add the tomatoes, filé, thyme and Cajun spice. Continue cooking until the mixture begins to stick to the pot. Add the roux, fish stock, parsley, okra, bay leaves and salt. Stir well and simmer for 1 hour.

CAJUN ROUX

Penned 'Cajun Napalm' by chef Paul Prudhomme, dark roux adds a unique taste and texture to Cajun food. There are roux ranging from medium brown to nearly black. Cooked with care, dark roux is an indispensable ingredient for use in soups and sauces.

Be careful though, because if it is splashed on your skin you'll have a nasty burn.....thus the name.

2 pounds medium shrimp,
  shelled and deveined
2 dozen oysters, shucked,
  with their liquor [optional]
1 pound crab claws
6 cups cooked white rice

Add the shrimp and crab claws and cook 10 minutes more. Just before serving add the oysters and return to simmer for 2 minutes.
Place a pile of rice in each shallow bowl and ladle the gumbo over it.

Baja Fish Tacos

The first time I encountered Baja tacos was while on a long road adventure through the peninsula. Right on the beach at Mulegé was an oasis of shade, seafood and cervesa. At small rusting tables set right on the sand plates of incredible fish and shrimp tacos wove their way to our table through rounds of beer and bowls of salsa...

FOR 12 TACOS
EQUIPMENT NEEDED:
POT WITH OIL FOR DEEP FRYING

1½ pounds fish filet: cod,
  snapper, grouper or rockfish
3 beaten eggs
¼ cup water
1 cup flour
¼ cup chile powder
1 teaspoon sea salt
canola oil for frying

12 corn tortillas
one half Santa Fe Slaw recipe,
  page 16
⅔ cup sour cream

Salsa Fresca, page 12

HEAT OIL IN FRYING POT TO 350°

Blend the flour with the chile powder. Cut the fish into 1 inch strips, 2 inches long. Pass the fish through the flour mixture, then into the beaten eggs and back into the flour to coat well. Fry the fish pieces until they are golden brown. Hold them warm while finishing all the fish.
Mix the Santa Fe Slaw with the sour cream.
Fry the corn tortillas for 10 seconds only. Drain them on paper towels. Fill each folded tortilla with fish and slaw. Serve with Salsa Fresca.

Note: Flour tortillas can be used. Don't fry them. Warm them only.

Skate Wings Braised in Sauvignon Blanc and Browned Butter

Skate is a highly respected fish in French cooking. While quite unusual to American tastes this recipe is famously popular when served at the A Bar A. Fresh skate doesn't come West regularly, however on the East coast it may be more available if your local seafood market takes it seriously. It is a very perishable fish that easily shows its age with an unmistakable odor of ammonia when past its prime. I strongly suggest good communication with your seafood provider, if not the trusty 'sniff' test before buying.

Note that skinless filets are called for in the recipe. The richness of this fish rivals that of lobster or scallops and its reasonable price makes it is one of the last great seafood values.

FOR EIGHT SERVINGS

2 sticks, ½ pound
  sweet butter
8 six ounce portions
  skinless skate filets
½ teaspoon kosher salt
½ cup flour
pinch white pepper

1 cup fish stock, page 30
⅔ cup Sauvignon blanc
2 tablespoons lemon juice
1 teaspoon kosher salt
¼ teaspoon white pepper
chopped parsley

PREHEAT OVEN TO 350°

Cook the butter in a small saucepan over medium-high heat until the foaming subsides and the milk solids begin to brown. Stir gently and cook until all the solids are browned, but NOT black. Remove from heat and hold the pan bottom in cold water for a few seconds to stop the cooking.

Dredge the lightly seasoned skate in flour and shake off the excess. In a heavy, oven proof pan heat 4 tablespoons of the browned butter. Cook the skate until golden brown. Turn the filets, add the stock, wine, lemon juice, salt and pepper. Cover loosely with foil and place the pan in the oven. Cook **10** minutes. Carefully remove the fish to a holding platter, cover them and keep warm.

Place pan over high heat and reduce the cooking liquid to ½ cup. While it is boiling, beat in the remaining browned butter. Spoon the sauce over the fish before serving. Garnish with the chopped parsley.

Filet of Salmon With Ginger - Orange Butter

Salmon is ever popular at the A Bar A as well as around the country. I have chosen this preparation because it is delicious with or without the sauce. Steaming offers a quick and healthful method of cooking fish. When the steam comes from quality wine or rich stock the fish benefits enormously. Don't hesitate to cook salmon and other seafood this way and serve them 'au naturel', without sauce. Steamed fish and seafoods are best served immediately after cooking. The interior of the filet should remain bright pink, *just* yielding to finger pressure when done.

SERVES SIX

GINGER-ORANGE REDUCTION
peeled zest of ½ orange
4 tablespoons chopped ginger
2 cups water
½ cup Champagne vinegar

Simmer the ginger, orange zest in the water and vinegar until reduced to ½ cup. Strain and hold this reduction for making the sauce.

6 six ounce salmon filets
½ cup dry white wine
⅓ cup fish stock
1 sprig fresh thyme
3 bay leaves
½ teaspoon kosher salt
pinch white pepper

Place the fish in a heavy non-reactive skillet with the wine, stock, herbs, salt and pepper. Bring barely to a sim-mer, cover and steam for about 10 minutes, depending on the thickness of the fish. Remove the fish and hold warm while the sauce is finished.

¼ pound softened sweet butter
½ cup heavy cream
¼ cup orange juice concentrate
¼ teaspoon sea salt
2 tablespoons chopped chervil
  or parsley

Reduce the liquid to ½ cup and add the *orange reduction,* the heavy cream the orange juice and the salt. Reduce over high heat to ½ cup, then off the heat quickly beat in the soft butter in small bits until absorbed. Spoon the sauce over the fish and garnish with the chervil.

Brochette of Cajun Sea Scallops Remoulade

The popularity of Cajun food swept the country and receded as fast as the storm surge of a Gulf of Mexico hurricane. However, true aficionados remain loyal fans of the unique blend of spices, aromatics and heat which is the trademark of Louisiana Cajun cooking.

The creative approach to their indigenous cuisine blended with a touch of Europe snagged me from the start. It's impossible to ignore this regional celebration of life as food, if food is your life.

This is a very simple way to enjoy Cajun flavors with scallops or shrimp. When buying sea scallops always look for 'dry-pack' scallops. Wet scallops are plumped in a mysterious liquid which is designed to extend their shelf life and increase their raw weight. Choose fairly large ones because they are easier to skewer. Always rinse and dry the scallops and remove the small, tough abductor muscle often found attached to the sides of scallops.

SERVES EIGHT

FOR THE REMOULADE SAUCE

4 hard cooked egg yolks

2 tablespoons Dijon mustard

½ cup diced celery

½ cup diced onion

½ cup diced green pepper

1 tablespoon minced garlic

2 tablespoons minced shallot

⅓ cup capers

½ cup chopped parsley

⅓ cup tomato paste

1 tablespoon fresh thyme leaves

3 tablespoons lemon juice

1 tablespoon Cajun Spice,
   page 41

1 tablespoon kosher salt

1½ cups mayonnaise

SPECIAL EQUIPMENT

Large Cast Iron Skillet

8 six inch bamboo skewers

Soak the bamboo skewers in water for 30 minutes.

PREPARE THE SAUCE

In a food processor blend the hard yolks with the mustard until smooth. Add all the remaining ingredients to processor and pulse to blend well. Add the mayonnaise and mix.

2 pounds sea scallops

2 tablespoons clarified butter

1 tablespoon flour

3 tablespoons Cajun Spice

3 tablespoons canola oil

Skewer the scallops through their sides, so they lay flat. Make eight skewers.

Blend the flour and Cajun Spice. Brush the scallops with clarified butter. Dredge in the spice mixture to coat evenly. Heat the skillet until very hot. Add the oil--it should almost smoke. Carefully place the brochettes in the skillet. Cook till browned on both sides. Scallops are done when they just spring back when pressed with a finger. Serve them on the skewer, placed *over* the Remoulade sauce with Basmati Rice Pilaf, page 64.

Cajun Spice Blend

¼ cup ground white pepper

¼ cup ground black pepper

2 tablespoons cayenne pepper

2 tablespoons onion powder

2 tablespoons garlic powder

1 tablespoons filé gumbo

¼ cup dry thyme leaves

½ teaspoon ground celery seed

Cajun Shrimp Remoulade

Use large white shrimp in place of the scallops. Remove the shells, except the tail section. Butterfly the shrimp by making a cut nearly through the back of the shrimp to remove any 'vein'. Proceed with the recipe for scallops remoulade, substituting shrimp.

Thai Grilled Shrimp

Perfect for the backyard grill, these shrimp will disappear amid the smacking sounds of collective fingers being licked. Serve as an appetizer or main course. The blend of flavors is definitely Oriental, but the addition of fresh basil and coconut milk directs your taste-buds to Thailand.

SERVES EIGHT AS AN APPETIZER

FOR THE MARINADE

1 cup chili sauce
1 tablespoon minced garlic
1 tablespoon minced ginger
1 teaspoon grated lime zest
⅓ cup chopped cilantro
⅓ cup brown sugar
¼ cup fish sauce*
¼ cup rice wine vinegar
⅓ cup coconut milk*
3 tablespoons chopped basil

3 pounds large shrimp
*Available at Asian groceries

Blend all the ingredients in a food processor. Peel the shrimp, leaving the tail intact. Butterfly the shrimp and remove the vein. Toss in the marinade to coat well and chill for at least 2 hours.

While best on a charcoal grill, these shrimp can be cooked in the broiler. The heat needs to be high enough to caramelize the coating. Shrimp cook fast when they are butterflied. Take care not to overcook them. They are done when the meat is opaque all the way through. Serve immediately.

A Visit to An Asian Grocery

One of the advantages of dabbling in Asian cooking is the adventure that awaits you when you shop at an Asian market for the necessary ingredients. There is just no substitute for the flavors captured in the imported jars and bottles found crammed onto the shelves there. Often devoid of any readable English, learn to trust the pictures on the labels to suggest the contents. You might stumble over buckets of unrecognizable foods and see certain parts of chickens for the first time. The aromas are pungent and memorable. Condiments include all manner of sauces, pastes and preserves. Be creative and buy with abandon for when you return home you'll have bags full of culinary surprises.

CHAPTER THREE

Chicken

and

Poultry

We serve a variety of poultry at the A Bar A Ranch including ducks, Guinea fowl, pheasant, quail, turkey and of course chicken.

The most common chicken found in supermarkets everywhere is a factory- raised bird that weighs about three pounds and is only 45 days old. How's that for fast growth! A bigger surprise is the fact that a three pound chicken has been fed less than 10 pounds of food during its lifetime...a very efficient critter.

We have a technologically advanced agri-business to thank for such remarkable statistics. We can also thank them for supplying low-cost, tasteless, antibiotic-laced, hormonal feats of science to our dinner table.

Fortunately, now there are alternatives. New brands of 'natural', or free range chicken can be found alongside the mass-market birds in stores everywhere. In our quest as consumers for better tasting foods, we created a market for cleaner production poultry that harkens back to the days when chicken had taste.

We tapped into the taste memories of family dinners when chicken was a proud culinary masterpiece...something that conjured up the image of field corn and whole grains.

Chickens are available in several sizes. [See following table] Back when barnyards contained raucous roosters, laying hens and chickens of every age we ate a larger variety of chickens. However, as we devote less time to cooking, most of the chickens sold are at the 3-4 pound stage. The demand for longer cooking birds like roasters and stewing hens has become limited. 'Fryers' come packaged whole or cut into pieces, inevery conceivable combination.

Modern chicken must be the most specialized food product designed for point of use. Parts are removed expressly for new and trendy markets, like wings for the hot wings bonanza or breast filets when fajitas went bonkers. Well, after all..." parts is parts."

I always recommend buying whole, fresh chicken. Cutting them up is not at all difficult. You can then freeze the parts not immediately needed. The cost benefit is tremendous and you will have a supply of scraps for stock or soup and leftovers for future meals..

Natural, organic or free-range birds are worth trying. They usually have a noticeably better taste. They in fact *have* taste. While they cost more than conventional chicken, they are well worth it. I am also a big fan of Kosher poultry. This is a market that produces specially bred, specially fed chickens and turkeys that definitely taste different from supermarket fowl.

While on the subject, I'd like to encourage buying eggs from small producers as well. They carefully choose the feed and offer fresher eggs with bright yolks and rich taste. If you are reducing your intake, even more the reason to treat yourself to better eggs. All this helps to support family farms and the families that own them- a necessary element of a healthy American agricultural landscape.

Chicken by any Name

	Age ------- Weight	Cooking Method	Serves	Comments
GAME HEN	21 Days ------- Under 1 Pound	Grill Roast	1	Usually frozen. Low meat-bone ratio Try Kosher version Good for stuffing
POUSSIN	30 Days --------- 2 Pounds	Grill Roast Saute	2	Availability limited Buy naturally-raised product Try Kosher product
BROILER	40 Days --------- 3 Pounds	Grill Roast Saute	2 - 3	Buy naturally-raised product Try Kosher product Great for quick roasting
FRYER	45 Days --------- 3 - 4 Pounds	Grill Roast Saute	2 - 4	Avoid mainstream products Buy fresh, 'free-range', local, Kosher or 'natural' product
ROASTER	75 Days --------- 4 - 6 Pounds	Roast Braise Saute Smoke	3 - 6	Try marinating, smoking Great for barbeque Good for stuffing
STEWING HEN	6 Months --------- 6 Pounds	Braise Boil	3 - 6	Needs long, moist cooking Product usually frozen

Tarragon Chicken

Soon after arriving in Paris for school, I ventured out into my new neighborhood to shop for my first homework project, Poulet à L'Estragon. I came home with more than chicken and tarragon. The chicken vendor asked what the chicken was for and proceeded to demonstrate how to precisely prepare his bird for the recipe. A stop for tarragon was a lesson in the intricacies of heating the herb to just the right temperature to release the aromas. It also netted me a 'better' recipe. A quick stop in the wine shop was a hard sell on the qualities of Chablis and how it is perfectly matched to the anise flavored overtones of tarragon. I returned home with a string bag holding a chicken, a bottle of wine, a bunch of tarragon and a dozen new friends.

Such was my neighborhood and so too were nearly all my shopping trips. Word spread that an American had come to learn how to cook and my neighbors were intent on doing the teaching.

SERVES SIX

6 *eight ounce boneless chicken breasts, skin on*
2 *tablespoons whole fresh tarragon leaves*
1 *teaspoon kosher salt*
¼ *teaspoon white pepper*
4 *tablespoons sweet butter*

2 *tablespoons chopped tarragon*
1 *cup dry white wine: French Chablis or Sauvignon Blanc*
3 *tablespoons chicken glace**
⅓ *cup heavy cream*
½ *teaspoon kosher salt*
¼ *teaspoon white pepper.*

Place whole tarragon leaves under the skin of the chicken. Carefully replace the skin to cover all the meat. Lightly salt and pepper the breasts. In a heavy sauté pan brown the chicken, skin side first in the butter. Remove the breasts from the pan and discard the butter. Deglaze the pan with the wine and chopped tarragon and replace the chicken to the pan. Cover and simmer for 15 minutes.

Remove the chicken and hold warm. Add the cream, salt and chicken glace and reduce to 1 cup. Spoon the sauce over the chicken and serve. The rich sauce requires a steamed potato or simple rice accompaniment.

The Best Roast Chicken and Vegetables

This chicken is toasty crisp on the outside, super juicy inside. The vegetables roast to a surprising sweetness. Choose fresh, top quality chickens-- natural, organic, or Kosher and be willing to roast at high temperature.

Prepare more vegetables than you think you'll need, as they disappear fast. Roast enough chickens to ensure leftovers--they make great sandwiches.

SERVES SIX

2 3-4 pound frying chickens
1 tablespoon kosher salt
½ teaspoon black pepper
4 sprigs fresh thyme
2 tablespoons olive oil

FOR THE VEGETABLES
6 medium carrots
18 baby new potatoes, halved
6 small onions, peeled, halved
6 parsnips
3 medium turnips
3 tablespoons olive oil
1 teaspoon kosher salt
½ teaspoon black pepper
2 cups chicken stock

PREHEAT OVEN TO 500°

EQUIPMENT NEEDED
LARGE ROASTING PAN

Dry the chicken with paper towels. Put salt, pepper and thyme inside the chickens. Trussing the chickens with cotton string is recommended, but not required. Secure the wings by folding them against the back with the neck skin underneath and rub the chickens with olive oil. Peel the carrots, parsnips, and turnips. Cut into 1 inch chunks. Add potatoes, onions, olive oil, salt, pepper and toss them in a bowl. Place the chickens in the roasting pan and surround them with the vegetables. The pan should be big enough so all fits snugly yet in a single layer.

Place in the middle of hot oven. Roast at 500° until chickens start to color lightly, about 20 minutes. Gently stir the vegetables. Turn oven down to 425°. Listen for sizzling and popping sounds...this is good- the French say: Il chant!... It's singing!

Check regularly to see that the vegetables are not burning. You can add some water or stock to slow their cooking. Nothing should burn in the pan. After about 50 minutes the chickens should be very brown, with bubbly, crisp skin. Remove from the oven and stab the thickest part of the thigh to check that the juices run clear. If you prefer WELL done joints, remove the vegetables and return the chickens to cook for 15 minutes more. Remove the chicken and hold warm. The resting period is important for easier carving.

Add the chicken stock to the roasting pan and over medium heat reduce to 1 cup while scraping the drippings. Strain and degrease the jus. Carve the whole breasts off the bone. Remove the thigh-leg quarters as well and arrange them on a serving platter with the vegetables. Serve the jus in a small pitcher.

Chicken Suprême Saltimbocca

Leave it to the Italians to create a dish that translates - 'Jump in your mouth'. While traditionally made with veal, we use chicken breasts for a creative variation.

FOR SIX SERVINGS

6 boneless, skin-on
  chicken breasts
6 thin slices prosciutto
6 slices provolone
18 fresh sage leaves
1 teaspoon kosher salt
½ teaspoon white pepper
3 tablespoons olive oil
1 cup rich chicken stock

PREHEAT OVEN TO 325°

Salt and pepper the chicken and place three sage leaves with a slice of prosciutto carefully under the skin. Heat the olive oil in a heavy, ovenproof saute pan and put the breasts in the pan, skin side down. Cook until browned. Turn over and brown other side. Remove the breasts from the pan. Add the stock and reduce by half. Replace the

chicken to the pan, skin up and place a slice of provolone on each. Finish cooking in the oven until the meat is done and the cheese is melted, about 10 minutes. Serve with simple pasta, tossed in olive oil with grated Asiago or Romano cheese.

Pollo Asada Yucateco

In towns throughout Mexico's Yucatan small streetside restaurants offer 'comida economica', which means cheap food. When pollo asado, or grilled chicken is the specialty, you can smell the aroma of your destination long before you see it. As with all great barbeque, the secret is the sauce, or in this case, the marinade.

In Mexico it is based on a blend of spices and annato bean paste, called achiote. A decent imported product can be found at specialty grocers. Grilling the marinaded chicken over a natural charcoal fire is ideal, but hardwood briquets are fine as well.

With plenty of warm corn tortillas, salsas and frijoles your guests can make their own tacos.

SERVES FOUR - SIX

SPECIAL EQUIPMENT NEEDED:
GRILL WITH CHARCOAL FIRE

4-5 *pound roasting chicken*

FOR THE MARINADE
1 *ounce Achiote* [dry weight]*
⅔ *cup orange juice*
⅓ *cup lime juice*
½ *cup chopped cilantro*
3 *cups sliced onions*
2 *tablespoons canola oil*
1 *tablespoon minced garlic*
1 *teaspoon oregano*
¼ *cup tequila*
2 *teaspoons kosher salt*

Cut the chicken through the backbone with kitchen shears or a sharp knife. Lay the chicken on a cutting board, skin side up. With a meat mallet or rolling pin firmly pound the chicken to flatten it. This helps the chicken cook evenly.

Cook the onions in the oil, stirring often until they are evenly browned, or caramelized. Blend the onions with the marinade ingredients in a food processor. Coat the chicken and cover to marinate in the refrigerator overnight.

Grill the chicken over medium coals turning frequently to cook evenly on both sides. The chicken is done when a meat thermometer inserted into the thickest part of the thigh reads 160°. Separate the legs, thighs and breasts which can be choppedinto two or three pieces. Arrange on a platter and serve with all the fixin's.

CHAPTER FOUR

Pasta

asta has been welcomed into our New American diet and is now universally enjoyed in infinite varieties. Once quite satisfied with soggy spaghetti noodles smothered in dull tomato sauce, we have evolved into discriminating fans of fusilli and farfalle.

We are easily overwhelmed with the myriad of flavors from chocolate to chipotle and there are at least 30 different dry cuts, or shapes to choose from. Flavor combinations like lemon-basil, black pepper-garlic or saffron-cardomon tempt us even further. Pasta is now made with whole wheat, corn, quinoa, spelt and artichoke flours. Oriental noodles are made with rice and buckwheat. The pastabilities are endless. We can't seem to get enough.

The ever-growing family of pasta includes all the filled varieties as well. Ravioli, tortellini and agnolotti are filled with meats, seafood, mushrooms and cheeses. Gnocchi, a potato-pasta dumpling has seen a recent return to menus as chefs search to offer every angle on the pasta rage. With all the innovation comes the need to understand and learn how to cook these new specialties. Some require a great deal of attention.

Pasta is sold fresh, frozen or dry, each different in their cooking method. Dry pasta requires longer cooking in boiling water than its fresh counterpart. Package directions will often suggest a cooking time, but usually these should be considered maximum times if firm or al dente pasta is desired. When precooking dry pasta for reheating later, less cooking time is required since reheating cooks the noodles further. I don't recommend precooking fresh pasta because it is very fragile when cooked and is easily broken.

One universal rule applies to all pasta-- cook it in plenty of boiling water, at least 6 quarts per pound to which 1 tablespoon coarse sea salt has been added. When fresh pasta is cooked, even more water is recommended since refrigerated noodles cool the water dramatically and quick reboiling of the water is crucial for proper cooking. Stir the pasta regularly, most importantly at the start to separate the noodles. Adding oil to the water can help to keep down foaming, but it can't prevent sticking during or after the cooking.

When precooking pasta for use at a later time undercook it slightly, then refresh it in cold water. Drain it well and toss it in some oil [2 tablespoons/pound]. Cooked pasta keeps well for 2 - 3 days in the refrigerator. Dropped in boiling water for 15 seconds and it's ready to serve. This step simplifies work in the kitchen when trying to put together a meal for several guests and timing is crucial.

Fresh pasta must be cooked just before serving. Use care not to overcook it or break the noodles during cooking. It usually cooks in less than 10 minutes, depending on the cut. Taste it often and when it is right, drain it quickly and serve. Make the sauces in advance.

Filled pastas like ravioli and tortellini require special handling to avoid breaking the pasta skin when cooking, stirring and draining. Always cook them in plenty of water and use wood or plastic utensils. Delicate raviolis should be skimmed out of the pot instead of poured through a colander when drained.

Frozen pasta is designed to be cooked while frozen. Don't thaw it prior to cooking. Ensure that the noodles separate fully in the water at the start of cooking. Take the same precautions as with fresh pasta.

We have come a long way in our appreciation of this Italian mainstay. Whether as an introduction to a multi-course feast or a main dish that stands alone, pasta can serve many purposes. Everybody loves it because it is versatile and simple, so there is no reason to settle for spaghetti and meatballs anymore.

Fettucine With Smoked Trout

In the style of 'Alfredo', this rich pasta dish is terrific as a starter, or as a lighter style main course when accompanied by a generous salad. A spicy Gewurztraminer from Sonoma Valley's Gundlach-Bundschu Winery is a perfect compliment to this fettucine's creamy and smoky sauce.

SERVES EIGHT

1 pound cooked fettucine
2 tablespoons minced shallots
2 tablespoons butter
2 cups heavy cream
⅛ teaspoon nutmeg
½ teaspoon kosher salt
ground white pepper
juice of ½ lemon
½ pound smoked trout filet
chopped chervil or parsley

Cook the shallots in butter until soft. Add the cream, salt, pepper and nutmeg. Reduce by half. Divide the smoked trout in two. Slice half into ¼ inch strips, cover and put them in the oven to heat through. Reserve this for the garnish. Break up the remaining smoked trout into bite-size pieces. Add trout pieces to the cream mixture heat well. Add the lemon juice and cooked fettucine to the saucepan. Toss gently to mix evenly. Garnish with the heated slices of trout and chopped chervil.

VARIATIONS

This preparation can be adapted by replacing the trout with any smoked fish, seafood or poultry. For another option add some saffron to the cream reduction or try adding chopped ripe tomatoes or caramelized shallots to the sauce. The pasta can be linguine, spaghetti, tagliatelle, or cappelini.

Be creative with recipes like this. Many possibilities evolve when you consider adding something different. Small amounts of meat or fish that alone wouldn't make a meal can be added to pasts and a simple sauce to serve several people. Often a glance in the refrigerator will launch an idea for a fresh invention.

Pesto Genovese

During the summer months in the gardens around the bustling Italian port city of Genoa, generous basil plants give themselves to the indispensable condiment known as pesto. From the Italian word for pestle, the tool traditionally used to grind the 'paste', pesto was originally simply tossed with hot pasta, but more recently has found its way onto pizza, in spreads, in marinades and as a component of sauces. The Provençal French embrace their own version, Pistou, which lacks pinenuts but is strong on nationalistic pride.

MAKES ONE CUP
½ cup basil puree*
3 tablespoons raw pinenuts
½ cup olive oil
2 tablespoons minced garlic
½ cup Parmigiano-Reggiano
1 teaspoon lemon juice
¼ teaspoon black pepper
1 teaspoon kosher salt

Puree basil leaves with oil to make the base. Add all the ingredients and puree until smooth. Be careful, overblending canblacken the basil. Always ensure there's a thin layer of oil protecting the pesto from the air and it will keep well for several days in the refrigerator.

ADDITIONS TO PESTO
Roasted red peppers
Sundried tomatoes
Roasted garlic
Oil cured olives
Anchovies

REPLACE BASIL WITH:
Arugula
Spinach
Cilantro
Watercress
Sorrel

Linguine al Pesto

While my childhood friends were sucking up long spaghetti noodles from a puddle of tomato sauce, at our family table my mother was tossing firm linguine with bright green, perfumed pesto. I learned from an early age that spaghetti sauce didn't have to be red. To this day I have a preference for pairing the aromatic opulence of pesto with linguine.

SERVES EIGHT

1½ pounds DeCecco linguine
⅔ cup pesto
shaved Parmigiano-Reggiano
fresh ground black pepper

Cook the pasta in salted water. Drain the linguine and toss it in a warmed bowl with the pesto. Serve with the shaved cheese and ground pepper

Orzo With Sundried Tomatoes

SERVES SIX

1 pound orzo pasta
2 tablespoons olive oil
¼ cup sundried tomatoes
   in oil, chopped
5 cups water
2 teaspoons kosher salt
chopped parsley or basil

Heat olive oil in a heavy saucepan. Add the orzo and cook while stirring until it just starts to color. Add the water, salt and tomatoes. Simmer very gently until water is absorbed.

Serve the orzo with a sprinkle of parsley.

Baked Penne With Gorgonzola

SERVES SIX-EIGHT
EQUIPMENT NEEDED:
8"x 10"x 2" baking dish

PREHEAT OVEN TO 350°

1 pound DeCecco penne, cooked
½ pound Gorgonzola
½ cup heavy cream
⅔ cup bread crumbs
¼ cup chopped Italian parsley
2 tablespoons minced garlic
3 tablespoons olive oil
1½ teaspoons kosher salt

Cook the garlic in the olive oil until soft. Add the parsley and bread crumbs, stir and set aside. Boil the cream in a saucepan and add the Gorgonzola. Stir to melt and add the pasta. Mix to coat well. Place in a buttered ceramic dish, sprinkle with the breadcrumb mixture and bake for 20 minutes.

Tagliatelle Siciliano

Tagliatelle falls between linguine and fettucine in thickness. Rich in the flavors and aromas of Southern Italy, this pasta sauce can be made quite quickly once all the ingredients are prepared.

SERVES SIX

1 pound DeCecco Tagliatelle, or equivalent dry pasta

1 large eggplant, in ½" cubes

1 teaspoon kosher salt

3 tablespoons olive oil

4 crushed garlic cloves

⅔ cup roasted, peeled and diced red pepper

3 cups peeled, seeded and diced ripe plum tomatoes

½ teaspoon ground black pepper

½ cup pitted and halved oil-cured black olives

4 tablespoons capers

12 filets of anchovies, chopped

10 large basil leaves, julienned

Sprinkle the eggplant with salt and drain off the bitter juices on a tilted plate or in a colander.

Heat the olive oil, add the garlic and cook until browned, then discard. Add the eggplant, peppers and black pepper. Cook till soft, about 15 minutes then add the tomatoes and anchovies. Simmer, covered for 20 minutes and add the olives, capers and basil. Toss and serve over hot pasta.

Angelhair With Warm Lobster in Its Liquor

This is an elegant presentation of a favorite seafood. It comes from a special menu series offered at La Chamaille Restaurant during the summer season, when France consumes large quantities of lobster. Chef Pierre Siri prepares a five course menu exclusively of lobster dishes, all surprisingly different and wonderfully creative. This one is perhaps the simplest to prepare in a home kitchen setting. You may need to call on your fishmonger to help with the preparation if cutting up a live lobster is difficult.

SERVES SIX

FOR THE LOBSTER LIQUOR

3 1½ pound live lobsters
1 leek, washed and chopped
3 ripe tomatoes, diced
2 celery stalks, diced
3 whole garlic cloves
3 sprigs fresh thyme
6 bay leaves
6 sprigs parsley or chervil
2 quarts fish stock
2 teaspoons kosher salt
8 whole peppercorns

1 pound DeCecco capellini
1 cup finely julienned leek,
   blanched 1 minute
1 cup diced seeded, peeled
   tomato
¼ pound sweet butter, soft
3 tablespoons chopped chervil
   or parsley

The lobsters are killed immediately with a knife plunged through the spinal cord directly behind the head. Separate the claws and the tail from the bodies. Remove any green matter from the tails.

Cut each body into 3 pieces and add them to the other ingredients in a saucepan and bring it to a simmer. Poach the tails and claws in the simmering broth for 12 minutes. Remove them to cool. Continue to simmer the liquor long enough to make 3 cups when strained.

Crack the claws and tails to remove the meat in whole pieces. Slice the tailmeat into round slices and hold it with the whole clawmeat in ½ cup of the warmed liquor.

Cook the capellini, drain and place it on the serving plates. Arrange the lobster on the pasta and decorate around the capellini with the blanched leek and diced tomato. Keep the plates warmwhile the sauce is made.

Bring the liquor to a quick boil and beat in the soft butter. Taste for salt. Spoon the sauce over the pasta and serve, garnished with chopped chervil.

CHAPTER FIVE

Potatoes

Rice

Beans

At the A Bar A we love our potatoes, rice and beans. Considered the staple foods of the frontier West, their heritage lives on in the hearts of comfort food lovers. While hard working cowboys may have been forced to subsist on basic starches, we have the advantage of enjoying them in countless ways as an accompaniment to many other foods.

There are hundreds of *potato* varieties grown around the world but until recently our markets were stocked with three or four kinds. Now more and more potatoes are being brought back to the market with great acceptance. It seems that we naturally long for certain traditional foods.

The same evolution is occuring with *beans*. Dozens of different beans can be found at any quality market. This has really expanded the possibilities for our menus at the A Bar A since beans are so representative of the Western experience.

No less a player in this renaissance of traditional foods is *rice*. It has been the principal diet of much of the world for centuries. Thanks to creative farmers around the country like the Lundberg's of California, exciting new varieties grace our plates and enhance our diets.

Garlic Smashed Potatoes

We call these popular, home-style potatoes 'smashed' because the skins are left on. We have tried every kind of potato for these. Our favorites are organic russets [bakers] and Yukon Golds. The russets have a grainier texture, while the Yukons tend to be creamier. These are very quickly made and wonderful. Add garlic to taste and leave plenty of lumps. There is one caution-- don't beat the cooked potatoes in a food processor because their starch, when overworked, becomes gluey and thick. Use a hand masher or a mixer with a paddle.

You can make these as rich as you want, however I prefer adding nonfat yogurt or buttermilk and just a little butter. The rich taste of our organically grown potatoes doesn't seem to need the addition of a lot of dairy fat.

FOR SIX - EIGHT SERVINGS

4 pounds potatoes
2 cups buttermilk or
  lowfat plain yogurt
3 tablespoons minced garlic
3 teaspoons kosher salt
1 teaspoon white pepper.

Cut the well washed potatoes into large chunks. Cook in salted water until soft. Drain the potatoes and mash with all the ingredients.

IDEAS FOR ADDITIONS TO THE POTATOES

Dark chile powder
Roasted garlic
Steamed fennel
Red pepper puree
Horseradish
Roquefort cheese
Caramelized onions
Powdered Ranch Dressing

Wild Rice With Sundried Cherries and Pistachios

This is a recipe for wild rice that adds elegance to roasted fowl and game meats entrees. The fruity crunchiness compliments the earthy flavors of the rice. This leftover rice can be transformed into wonderful little pancakes, page 66.

INGREDIENTS FOR EIGHT
SERVINGS

1½ cups wild rice

3 cups water

1 teaspoon sea salt

2 tablespoons butter

1 onion, quartered

FOR BOUQUET GARNI

2 three inch celery stalks

small bunch parsley

2 large bay leaves

2 sprigs thyme

white cotton string

⅓ cup shelled, coarsely chopped pistachio nuts

½ cup dried tart cherries

2 tablespoons minced shallots

1 teaspoon chopped fresh sage

1 tablespoon butter

pinch kosher salt

pinch black pepper

Put the wild rice in a saucepot with the water, salt, butter and onion. Tie the bouquet garni herbs tightly between the celery stalks and place it in the pot with the rice. Cook at a gentle simmer until the rice 'pops' completely. Like popcorn the insides of each grain become the outside. Ideally it will be all popped when the water is cooked away, but if not, add small amounts of water until the rice is all popped. Remove the bouquet garni and the onion. Drain and hold the rice warm.

Cook the pistachios in the butter until lightly golden, then add the shallots. Cook two minutes more, until the shallots are soft. Add the dried cherries, sage and the rice. Season to taste and hold covered for 5 minutes before serving.

French Lentils

Of the three most readily available varieties of lentils: red, green and French, my favorite is the French. The small dark green legumes remain firm when cooked and have a full, rich flavor. Look for these

at markets with large imported foods departments and in finer
health food stores.

FOR SIX SERVINGS

1½ cups french lentils
1 peeled carrot, cut in pieces
1 medium onion, cut in quarters
4 inch bouquet garni
1 tablespoon tomato paste
2 teaspoons kosher salt
5 cups light stock

Place all the ingredients in a saucepan. Bring to a gentle simmer and
cook for about 45 minutes, until the
lentils are soft. Add water as needed
if the level drops below the lentils.
Let stand for 15 minutes prior to
serving. Discard the bouquet garni
and the vegetables. The lentils can
be served with or without their
cooking broth.

Portabello and Shiitake Mushroom Risotto

This is a wonderful dish redolent with the earthy taste and aroma
of meaty portabellas and delicate shiitakes. Both of these mushrooms
are becoming easy to find in markets everywhere. While perfect as a
rich accompaniment to hearty main courses, risotto can be served as
a principal dish whenever a single entree is desired. Allow about 30
minutes attentive cooking time for risotto and serve it immediately.
Use only arborio rice, usually imported from Italy.

SERVES SIX - EIGHT

STOCK FOR COOKING THE RICE

3 quarts light stock: veal,
    chicken or vegetable
4 inch bouquet garni
1 pound portabellas, sliced
1 pound shiitakes, stemless
1 tablespoon minced garlic
4 tablespoons olive oil
1 tablespoon kosher salt

Slice the shiitake caps. In a heavy
soup pot heat the olive oil and cook
the seasoned mushrooms over high
heat until browned. Add the garlic,
the bouquet garni, stock and salt.
Simmer for 30 minutes. Remove the
bouquet garni.

2 cups arborio rice
2 tablespoons olive oil
¼ cup minced shallots
2 teaspoons kosher salt
½ teaspoon black pepper
truffle oil [see glossary]
3 tablespoons chopped parsley
shaved romano cheese

In a heavy bottomed saucepan cook the rice in the olive oil for 2 minutes over low heat. Add the shallots and cook for one minute more. Add enough simmering stock with mushrooms to barely cover the rice. Season with salt and pepper. Adjust the heat to maintain a gentle simmer. Cook while stirring until the liquid is almost absorbed. Add more stock and repeat - cooking and stirring until rice becomes creamy and cooked just to tender. Boiling water can be substituted if you run out of stock. Don't overcook. The rice shoudn't be mushy. Season with salt and pepper. Stir in the parsley and serve with shaved Romano cheese.

Gratin Dauphinois

The foothills region of Eastern France celebrates its agricultural bounty with this simple and wonderfully rich potato gratin. Comté cheese resembles Swiss Gruyère. Its nutty sweetness blends beautifully with the cream, garlic and nutmeg. Bubbly and browned, Gratin Dauphinois is a classic tribute to the lush, green pastures and rolling hills of Franche-Comté.

FOR EIGHT SERVINGS
SPECIAL EQUIPMENT NEEDED
8"x 10"x 2" baking dish,
   preferably ceramic

3 pounds peeled russet potatoes
2 cups heavy cream
1 teaspoon minced garlic
½ teaspoon nutmeg
1 cup grated Comté, Gruyère,
   Jarlsberg or Emmenthaler
2 teaspoons kosher salt
½ teaspoon white pepper

PREHEAT OVEN TO 375°
Hold whole peeled potatoes in water to prevent browning.
The potatoes should be thinly and uniformly sliced. A 'mandoline' or Japanese slicer is very helpful for this job if your knife skills aren't up to it. Once sliced, potatoes brown quickly when left exposed to the air so it is important to have all the ingredients ready to assemble before beginning.
In a small saucepan bring the cream,

garlic, salt, pepper and nutmeg to a simmer. Cool slightly and pour into the baking dish.

Slice the potatoes 1/16 inch thick, directly into thecream mixture. Layer them evenly to a depth of 1 inch. Press firmly to pack them tightly. Top with the grated cheese. Wipe the rim and place in the oven. Adjust temperature to 350° and bake for about 30 minutes. Move the dish to an upper rack and cook 20 minutes more. Test with a small sharp knife plunged into the center. There should be no resistance. If the cheese is not yet browned, pass under the broiler for a few seconds. The gratin will hold for an hour before serving. Hold very warm.

In Europe the best quality of some cheese is considered seasonal. Since the richest milk is produced when milk cows eat young shoots of springtime grass, cheese made from spring milk has the finest taste. Therefore, cheeses like Comté, Gruyère, Emmenthaler and Jarlsberg which are aged for about 3 months taste best when eaten in late summer.

Indian Spiced Creamed Potatoes

Substitute peeled and sliced yams for half the potatoes in the preceding recipe. Replace the garlic and nutmeg with 1/4 teaspoon each *ground cardamon, cinnamon, cloves* and *coriander.* Layer the yams between two layers of potatoes. Omit the cheese and proceed as described above.

The Secrets to Cooking Perfect Rice

Cooking rice successfully requires close attention to a few details. The rice, the pot and the cooking method all contribute to making great tasting rice that is perfect every time. It is important to know the rice you are working with. Rices differ greatly in taste, water requirements and in their cooking times. I choose to cook Basmati exclusively when I want long grain white rice. It has uniform grains and an aromatic quality that tastes nutty. Generally, white rice needs to be rinsed before cooking because when the grains rub during storage they produce powder that makes the rice gummy. However, the most common cause of sticky rice is starting with too much water. Read the packaging for a suggested amount of water to use. Often this will need adjusting, but it is a good place to begin.

Choose your cookware carefully. While an electric rice cooker is ideal, a heavy pot with a tight lid works well. Since rice is being steamed when it is cooked, the vapor must be trapped within the pot, over low heat as a rule. A very important part of successful rice cooking is trust. Once the lid is placed on the pot and the heat is adjusted, you must **not** remove it until the rice is cooked! Not even a peek or valuable steam is lost and the rice will cook unevenly. After cooking for the suggested time remove the pot from the heat and let it rest for 15 minutes, undisturbed. Then you can open the pot and fluff the rice with a fork.

The first two or three times you cook a brand of rice take note if too much water was used - swollen, mushy grains; or if too little-- dry, undercooked grains. Make the adjustment and try again. If the rice cooks unevenly it usually means that some steam escaped due to a loose lid. Try using a piece of foil under the lid. If the rice is crusty brown on the bottom, this usually means the cooking was too long or the temperature too high.

After a couple tries you will know the rice and you can trust that it will cook right each time. It helps to always use the same pot and lid once you succeed and stay with a brand of rice that you can regularly find.

Basmati Rice Pilaf

This is a classic French version of white rice cooked with onions and butter. While traditionally cooked in the oven, this aromatic pilaf is easily prepared on the stove.

SIX SERVINGS

1 cup basmati rice
2 tablespoons butter
½ cup diced onion
2 sprigs fresh thyme
4 bay leaves
1½ cups water
2 teaspoons kosher salt

Basmati is an aromatic rice whose flavor intensifies with aging. It is a premium choice among rice lovers the world over. The best Basmati rice is from Thailand and India.

Wash rice under cool water until the water runs clean. Drain well. In a heavy pot with a tight lid cook the onions until soft. Add the rice, salt, thyme, bay leaves and water. Bring to a simmer. Stir once, place the lid on the pot, and turn down the heat to LOWEST setting. Steam for 30 minutes.

Take off the heat. Let the rice rest *undisturbed* for 10 minutes.

Remove the lid and discard the thyme and bay leaves. Fluff with a fork and serve.

Indian Rice

Omit the onions, thyme and bay leaves from the previous recipe. Add 8 whole green cardamom pods, 6 cloves, 8 whole peppercorns and a 4 inch stick of cinnamon. Cook the rice the same way and remove the spices before serving.

Saffron Rice

Either of the two preceding recipes can be adjusted by adding several saffron threads to the water before cooking.

Mexican Green Rice

Omit the thyme and bay from the basic recipe. In a food processor puree ⅔ cup chopped cilantro, 2 teaspoons cumin, 1 jalapeño pepper and 2 anaheim peppers, both seeded. Add enough water to this mixture to make the 1½ cups liquid called for in the recipe. Cook the rice in the same way.

Ranch Roast New Potatoes

Potatoes more than all other vegetables best reflect the efforts of organic growing methods. Organic potatoes taste of the fertile earth in which they are grown. Commercial potatoes are bland and uninteresting because they are grown for weight, uniformity and storability instead of taste.

Fortunately some farmers have renewed their lands to produce potatoes proud enough to boast their French name--'apple of the earth'. I urge you to locate organic potatoes worthy of such praise. It will bring excitement to your table as no other simple food can.

SERVES EIGHT

3 pounds new or baby potatoes,
  left whole
kosher salt
4 tablespoons olive oil
2 teaspoons kosher salt
½ teaspoon black pepper
6 whole garlic cloves

2 teaspoons chopped rosemary
2 teaspoons chopped thyme

PREHEAT OVEN TO 400°
SPECIAL EQUIPMENT :
HEAVY ROASTING PAN

Wash the potatoes and cook them in salted water until **almost** tender. Drain and toss them with the olive oil, salt, pepper and garlic. Roast in the oven for 20 minutes, gently stirring occasionally. Reduce the temperature to 325°, add the herbs and cook the potatoes for 20 minutes more until browned and creamy soft in the center. Serve immediately.

Celery Root Puree

Celeriac, or celery root is highly esteemed in Europe, where it may be found served raw on a crudité salad, or treated as other root vegetables. To prepare this recipe trim off the dirt-encrusted skin and roots. Inside is creamy white, with an aromatic celery flavor that is mild and sweet. Treat the celery root like the potatoes in this recipe. The best method for pureeing is with a potato ricer, because the starch in the potatoes shouldn't get overworked. Another option is to remove only the celery root and puree it alone in a food processor since it is too fibrous to mash by hand, then add them to the potatoes which have been mashed separately.

SERVES EIGHT

SPECIAL EQUIPMENT NEEDED
POTATO RICER OR FOOD MILL

3 *pounds russet potatoes,*
   peeled and cut into 2" dice

1 *pound celery root, peeled*
   and cut into 2" dice

2 *teaspoons kosher salt*

2½ *cups warm milk*

¼ *pound unsalted butter*

½ *teaspoon kosher salt*

½ *teaspoon white pepper*

Cover the celery and potatoes with water, add salt and cook until tender. Drain well. Pass the potatoes and celery root through a ricer directly back into the cooking pot. Add the milk and butter. Stir well while heating. The consistency should be softer than normal mashed potatoes.

Sweet Onion and Potato Puree

Use sweet onions: Vidalia, Walla Walla or Maui Sweets in place of the celery root. Follow the same preparation.

Parsnip and Potato Puree

Substitute parsnips for the celery root and proceed the same way.

Carrot and Potato Puree

Substitute carrots for the celery root in the preceeding recipe.

Leek and Potato Puree

Substitute cleaned and chopped leeks for the celery root in the preceeding recipe. Boil them with the potatoes.

Wild Rice Pancakes With Fresh Sage

Use the wild rice from the recipe on page 59. These small cakes keep well for up to 30 minutes if wrapped in a tea towel and held warm. They are a great accompaniment to roasted meats. Serve them underneath medallions, quail, or game meats for a great looking presentation.

MAKES ONE DOZEN PANCAKES
4 cups cooked wild rice
4 tablespoons minced shallots
2 teaspoons chopped fresh sage
3 large eggs, separated
4 tablespoons flour
1 teaspoon baking powder
3 tablespoons canola oil

Separate the eggs. Put the whites into a bowl for beating later, see page 98. Blend the flour and the baking powder. Mix the yolks with the riceAdd the cooked rice, shallots and sage. Add the flour mixture while stirring. Beat the egg whites to stiff peaks. Gently fold them into the rice. Heat the oil in a heavy sauté pan. Drop the rice mixture from a spoon to form pancakes about 4 inches wide, using the spoon to spread the mixture. Cook over moderate heat until lightly browned. Turn over and cook remaining side. Hold warm until served.

Polenta Colorado

This delicious polenta can be served piping hot or chilled and grilled. Blending Tex-Mex spices and full flavored peppers helps to create a versatile and easy to prepare side dish....perfect with chicken or pork entrees.

If you want to grill it, spread it ¾ inch thick on an oiled baking sheet while it is still hot. Once cooled it can be cut into shapes, brushed with oil and grilled over a hot fire or pan fried.

FOR EIGHT SERVINGS
½ cup diced red pepper
⅓ cup roasted, peeled and diced
   poblano pepper
1 cup diced onion
1 tablespoon minced garlic
2 tablespoons canola oil
½ teaspoon cumin
2 tablespoons chile powder
2 teaspoons kosher salt
3 cups chicken or vegetable
   stock
1 cup instant polenta

Cook the onions, red pepper, garlic and poblanos in the oil until tender, about 5 minutes. Add the spices, salt and stock. Bring the mixture to a boil.

Slowly pour the polenta into the simmering stock mixture, while stirring, to avoid lumps. Cook for 5 minutes over low heat. Cover and keep warm until served. If the polenta thickens too much, stir in a little warmed stock or water.

Potato Tourte 'La Chamaille'

La Chamaille was a popular Paris restaurant for musicians and artists during the 70's. Located on the Ile St. Louis, this quiet 'atelier' of cutting-edge French cuisine was my classroom when I studied in Paris. Pierre and Raymonde Siri served this rich potato tourte to their guests nightly. Whenever I reminisce of the incredible years spent under Pierre's guidance, I whip up not only this tourte, but many fond souvenirs as well.

SERVES EIGHT
EQUIPMENT NEEDED

9"x 2" round cake pan
12 ounces puff pastry*
1½-2 pounds thinly sliced
Russet potatoes
2 teaspoons kosher salt
¼ teaspoon white pepper
¼ teaspoon nutmeg
1 cup heavy cream

PREHEAT OVEN TO 350°

Roll out the pastry to a 16 inch circle, roughly. Line the cake pan with the pastry, the extra dough hanging over the rim. Fill the pan with the potato slices, in layers, adding salt, pepper and nutmeg as you reach the top edge. Fold the overhanging pastry back over the potatoes all around to envelope the potatoes completely. Bake for 45 minutes, until lightly browned. Remove from the oven and cut a 4 inch diameter circle out of the pastry top. Slowly pour the cream into the tourte. Replace the pastry circle and bake 30 minutes more. Let it rest for 30 minutes out of the oven before cutting into wedges for serving.

* Puff pastry can be found in the freezer case of grocery stores.

Suggestion

The tourte can be easily made into a main course with the addition of julienned, cooked meat: country ham, roast lamb or beef, even smoked salmon or trout. Try adding fresh herbs or some roasted garlic puree to the cream before filling the crust.

On Cooking Beans...

There is a debate ongoing about the need to soak dry beans before cooking them. My experience has shown that under normal conditions: when cooking at near sea level and using reasonably fresh beans there is no need to soak the beans. Soaking does save cooking time when at elevation. However, when faced with an unusually stubborn batch of beans no amount of soaking or cooking can soften the starch to the creamy consistency desired of fully cooked beans. This is a rare occasion that I have mostly eliminated by purchasing beans from health food stores and reputable markets where the beans haven't been on the shelves for months or years.

The other debate concerns whether to salt beans while they cook. I firmly believe in salting the water for all vegetables, pasta, rice and legumes, including beans. I prefer salting food **during** cooking so the interior is properly seasoned from the start. It is claimed that salting beans while cooking toughens the skins. I don't find that to be the case.

Frijoles Charros [Cowboy Beans]

This is a basic pinto bean preparation that can be made with or without meat. These beans can be served as is or used in a variety of other ways. We make frijoles refritos, baked beans, Slim's Beans and bean soup from this base recipe.

SERVES EIGHT-TEN
1 pound cleaned pinto beans
1 large onion, halved,
   with root attached,
2 smoked pork hocks
1 cup tomato puree
8 whole garlic cloves
6 bay leaves
1 teaspoon oregano leaves
2 tablespoons Kosher salt
3 quarts water

Put all the ingredients into a large heavy bottomed pot and simmer for 1½-2 hours, until the beans are tender. The meat can be pulled off the bone and added to the beans or it can be removed. Discard the bay leaves. The broth should be slightly thick. Add more water as necessary.

Slim's Beans

Long before A Bar A country was familiar to us it was the home of a quiet, gritty homesteader called Slim. He raised a small cabin at the edge of a grove of Aspens in a draw leading down to the North Platte River. Remains of his home exist to this day and his final resting place was recently discovered not far from the location of our Slim's Draw dinner ride. He has quite a view...

SERVES EIGHT-TEN

Charro beans, preceding recipe	In a large, heavy sauce pan cook the
1 pound smoked bacon	bacon until almost crisp. Add the
2 cups tomato sauce	onions and cook until soft. Add the
2 cups diced onion	beans and the other ingredients.
2 cups brown sugar	Simmer gently for one hour, stirring
1½ cups molasses	occasionally to keep the beans from
½ teaspoon cayenne	sticking to the bottom.

Creamy Polenta

Polenta is becoming more popular as interest in Italian foods continues to diversify. There are two kinds of polenta available: quick cooking and regular. I have a preference for the regular because the grains are better defined. Because regular polenta takes 15 minutes of constant stirring, there are times when the instant version is very convenient.

SERVES SIX	Bring stock and seasonings to a boil.
6 cups light stock or water	Add the polenta in a steady stream
1½ cups regular polenta	while stirring to prevent lumps.
2 teaspoons kosher salt	Turn down the heat to gently
2 bay leaves	simmer and stir while cooking for
4 whole garlic cloves	15 minutes. The constant stirring is
4 tablespoons sweet butter	necessary to make the polenta
½ cup grated Romano cheese	creamy. If using an aluminum pan
	use a wooden spoon so the polenta

doesn't discolor. It is done when it is creamy and the grains are tender to taste. Remove the garlic cloves and bay leaves. Stir in the butter and cheese. Serve immediately or cover and adjust the consistency right before serving.

CHAPTER FIVE

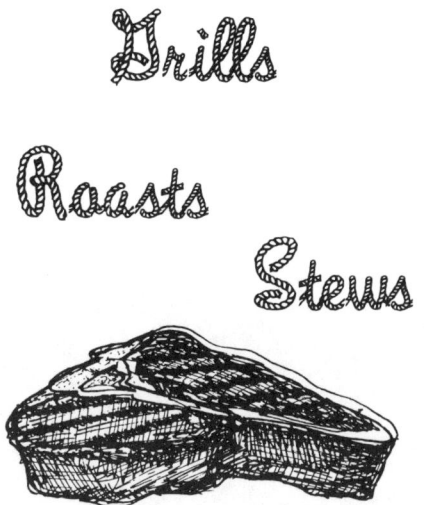

Grills
Roasts
Stews

A s they wind their way down the Ranch road upon arriving at the A Bar A, our guests may encounter many cattle...sometimes a bit too closely. Many presume that they are meeting a future dinner. Although there are thousands that graze and roam our widely defined property, circumstances are such that they won't be served in the ranch's dining room.

A Bar A cattle are raised for a large national market. They are trucked away to feedlots prior to slaughter and processed at facilities far from Wyoming. It is virtually impossible to keep track of our cattle once they leave our property. While we are certainly proud of our stock, until they are slaughtered we wouldn't know if they make the grade. All the beef served at the A Bar A is Angus, a breed selected for its superior eating qualities.

After beef is slaughtered it is graded. There are three prominent grades pertinent to this discussion and many more that don't concern us. The top three are Prime, Choice and Select, in descending order of 'quality'. Simply put the higher the fat content, seen as marbling, the higher the grade. The marbling is a result of many factors. The most obvious is the period of time spent in the feedlot eating corn and other high quality feed. Since this 'fat farm' is an expensive visit the higher the grade, the more expensive the meat.

We buy beef selected from the top end of the choice grade. It has been carefully aged by our purveyor and then by us. Aging is the process of tenderizing and flavor enhancement brought about over time by the natural enzymes present in the meat itself. We take great pride in the beef served at the A Bar A Ranch. With better under-standing of the product and the market you can buy the same beef as we do for your dining at home.

How to Buy Great Tasting Beef

Much is being reported regarding the place of beef in our ever-changing diet. Most of this revolves around health concerns and questions about quality. I often hear complaints about the beef sold in our supermarkets. Many people feel that generally the quality, and specifically the taste and tenderness of the beef they buy has dropped significantly in the past several years. There is no question that factors have impacted the industry in ways few people foresaw.

Our zeal for a lowfat diet and the fact that beef consumption in the U.S. fell in the 80's resulted in a concerted effort on the part of both the beef industry and the government to change the way they did business. They ran a huge media blitz to counter the perception that beef was unhealthy. Their claims were backed up by the intro-duction of leaner cattle. Under previous circumstances these leaner steers wouldn't have had the necessary fat to grade well enough to bring in desired profits so the meat packers persuaded the govern-ment to ease their standards, allowing leaner cattle to grade out higher. There was no argument from consumers because we had asked for a healthier diet, including less fat.

Today we have meat counters filled with leaner meat that may not have been 'good' enough for supermarket shelves fifteen years ago. The lower fat content and younger age of the steers has resulted in tougher, less flavorful beef in general.

Throughout this adjustment period finer steak restaurants very patiently hung around for customers who longed for the well marbled, old fashioned beef. Eventually we discovered that great beef was still available if we went out to eat. What was once accessible to all consumers now was restricted to those who could afford the specialty establishments that served it.

The newest marketing thrust is underway. The gourmet grocery industry is booming with national chains saturating our cities with healthy competition for our food dollar. This also is a result of our request for a better diet. These new markets offer better beef, not only the 'natural' brands. Look for Certified Angus Beef at choice grade or better and you will enjoy the same quality as we serve at the A Bar A . Expect to pay a premium for this specialty beef but stiff competition benefits the consumer and there are plenty of stores out there.

Choosing the Right Cut

Better understanding of how certain parts of the steer differ helps you to choose the right cut of beef. The more an animal's muscles work the greater the blood flow and therefore the richer the flavor. So while fat content relates to tenderness and juiciness, also look to consider all the qualities before deciding on a certain cut.

Perhaps the most important factor is choosing the right cooking method to match the cut. There are only a few options. The quickest are grilling and sauteing. These are generally reserved for cuts that are tender by virtue of their lack of work: sirloin, tenderloin and rib. Roasting has many more possibilities including all of the above and parts of the shoulder [chuck] and the hind quarter [round]. Longer cooking techniques like stewing and braising are chosen for the hardest working parts of the animal. These include some of the above and the flank, shank, neck, brisket and rump.

Usually the tenderest cuts are the most expensive. However when rich taste and lower fat is desired the less costly cuts are a great choice. I've included recipes for some of these options because I prefer meats with full flavor.

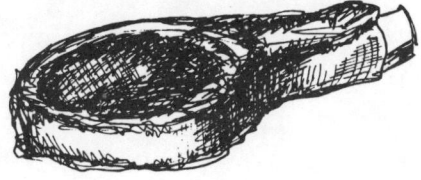

Grilled Marinated Flank Steak

Flank steak is very challenging and satisfying to prepare. It is potentially a very tough cut if overcooked or carved incorrectly. The grain is very well defined and requires thin carving against or perpendicular to this grain.

The marinade in this recipe caramelizes over hot coals and becomes sweet and crunchy. I recommend cooking only up to medium temperature because flank steak becomes tough and dry beyond that, unless it is braised for a considerably longer time.

FOR SIX SERVINGS
4-5 pound flank steak

SPECIAL EQUIPMENT NEEDED
CHARCOAL GRILL

FOR THE MARINADE
½ cup tomato ketchup
⅓ cup worcestershire sauce
¼ cup brown sugar
⅛ cup shoyu
¼ cup molasses
1 tablespoon minced garlic
1 tablespoon Dijon mustard
1 teaspoon cayenne [optional]
2 teaspoons black pepper
1 tablespoon kosher salt

Blend all the marinade ingredients. Stir well to dissolve the brown sugar.

Brush a heavy coat on both sides of the flank steak. Reserve some to serve with the steak. Cover and refrigerate for at least 2 hours. Prepare a hot charcoal grill. Cook the flank steak over moderately hot coals. For the average flank steak figure about 7-10 minutes per side. Light char on the surface is desired, but don't burn OFF the marinade. Remember the steak will continue to cook further while off the heat, so don't overcook it. Carve the flank at a severe angle from top to bottom, starting at the widest end. Cut thin slices across the grain at least 2 inches wide. This is very important or the meat will be chewy. Some reserved marinade can be served alongside or brushed on before carving.

Slow Roasted Prime Rib of Angus Beef

The expectations for our prime rib are perhaps higher than for anything else we cook regularly at the A Bar A Ranch. It is part of our Saturday night 'cowboy formal' dinner tradition.

The success of something as straightforward as prime rib depends heavily on the quality of the beef, so don't skimp. Ribs can be bought with or without bones. Bone-in roasts shrink less and the bones can be enjoyed as leftovers or stock makings, however they are more difficult to carve. Boneless prime rib roasts are called ribeyes.

I prefer slow roasting, for about 10 minutes per pound for boneless ribeye and a little longer for bone in. Always use an accurate thermometer to verify. Roasts continue cooking outside the oven and they need a rest period prior to carving to 'equalize' and relax.

SPECIAL EQUIPMENT NEEDED
Large roasting pan

FOR SIX 10 -12 OUNCE
SERVINGS

4 - 5 pound *Ribeye roast*
⅓ *cup kosher salt*
¼ *cup ground black pepper*
2 *carrots, cut into pieces*
2 *stalks celery, cut in pieces*
1 *onion, quartered*
2 *cups beef or veal stock*

Creamy Horseradish Sauce
1 cup sour cream
⅓ cup prepared horseradish
1 teaspoon minced garlic
1 teaspoon kosher salt
¼ cup chopped parsley

PREHEAT OVEN TO 325°

Let the beef come to room temperature. Place the vegetables in the roasting pan. Mix the salt and pepper and coat the meat. Place it on the vegetables fat side up and roast it for 45 minutes - 1 hour. Insert the thermometer into the center of the roast and read the temperature. Remembering that the roast will cook further after removing it from the oven, take it out at:

115°--Rare
120°--Medium rare
125°--Medium
130°--Well

Cover it with foil to keep warm. Cook on medium heat while stirring to caramelize the drippings without burning them. Carefully pour off the clear fat. Add the stock and reduce by ⅓ while scraping the pan. Strain the jus and skim off the fat. Carve the roast and serve 'au jus'.

Wyoming Beef Stew and Cookie's Biscuits

When late Wyoming summers turns cool, we answer the farewell to hot days and warm ranch evenings by serving comfort foods like this rich, meaty stew with biscuits accompanied by the crackle of the hearth's first fire of the season.

The shoulder, or chuck is the best choice for stews since they require fairly long cooking. The chuck remains moist, unlike other cuts like round steak which become dry and chewy after an hour of braising. Precut supermarket stewing beef can contain pieces from different cuts, so the cooking is uneven, resulting in some pieces being tough and others tender. The butcher can cut up the large chuck steak if you don't feel comfortable with the job.

Often stews have only the remnants of vegetables left because they were cooked as long as the beef. We always precook the vegetables separately and add them at the end so that they remain whole and colorful.

SERVES SIX

SPECIAL EQUIPMENT

large ovenproof pot with lid

3 *pounds chuck roast,*
    cut into 1½ inch pieces

4 *tablespoons canola oil*

1½ *teaspoons kosher salt*

1 *teaspoon black pepper*

1½ *cups diced onions*

1½ *cups diced celery*

4 *whole garlic cloves*

5 *tablespoons flour*

⅔ *cup canned crushed tomatoes*

2 *cups diced plum tomatoes*

2 *tablespoons tomato paste*

3 *cups rich beef stock*

4 *bay leaves*

2 *teaspoons rubbed sage*

PREHEAT OVEN TO 225°

Season the beef and cook it at medium-high heat until well browned. Turn the pieces only as they brown. If the pieces are moved around too much they steam in the pan instead of browning. Remove the beef as it's browned and reduce the heat so the pan glaze **doesn't** burn. Add the onions, celery and garlic. Stir and scrape the pan glaze as the vegetables soften. Add the cooked meat pieces [save the juice] and the flour. Cook while stirring until the flour absorbs the fat. Add the tomatoes, stock, tomato paste, meat juices and herbs. Cover and place in the oven. Cooking time depends on the size of the meat pieces. Begin checking

PREPARING THE VEGETABLES

1½ cups whole baby carrots

2 cups skin-on baby potatoes

1½ cups celery, peeled, cut into
   2 inch pieces and blanched

1 cup pearl onions, peeled
   and blanched

1 tablespoon butter

1 tablespoon sugar

1½ cups small mushrooms

¼ cup water

1 teaspoon lemon juice

½ teaspoon kosher salt

pinch white pepper

1 tablespoon butter

Storing Hint

We have all tasted a stew dish as a leftover and felt it tasted better the next day. Why is that? Because the meat relaxes and the flavors marry. If you make this stew to serve the next day, store the vegetables and the meat separately, with some sauce on each. Gently reheat the more fragile vegetables and the meat in separate pans and combine them afterwards. The vegetables will remain whole and attractive.

---

after one hour. The stew should not boil, just barely simmer.

Blanch the carrots until tender, then drain them and hold.

Slightly undercook the potatoes in boiling water, drain and reserve covered.

Carefully peel the onions, leaving the root trimmed, but attached. Blanch until tender. Drain and saute in butter and sugar until glazed golden. Set aside.

Peel off the strings from large celery stalks with a vegetable peeler. Cut them diagonally and blanch them in boiling water for 5 minutes. Refresh in cold water and drain.

Cook the mushrooms in salted water with the lemon and pepper for 10 minutes, covered. Drain and add the juices to the stew. Saute the mushrooms in the butter until browned. Set aside.

When the stew meat tests done, after about 1½ hours, remove the pieces and hold them warm. Strain the sauce. Combine the vegetables with the meat and add the sauce. Heat gently and adjust the salt and pepper as needed. Serve with Cookie's Biscuits on page 84.

Rack of Lamb Provençale with Roasted Vegetables

The lamb served at the A Bar A is carefully chosen Colorado lamb which is mild in flavor and not too large. We trim off most of the fat and season it generously with garlic, fresh herbs and extra virgin olive oil. The racks are first cooked on the broiler and then finished in the oven. Equally good results can be achieved cooking them in a conventional oven without any grilling.

We serve a three or four bone rack -- each full rack has seven ribs and we halve them. We remove nearly all the cap fat, leaving only a thin layer for protection during grilling. The meat between the ribs is removed, called 'Frenching', then the fat layer is scored which helps to hold the seasonings and garlic. With the addition of lavender and a fruity olive oil we are reminded of the virtues of Provençale French cuisine...toujours.

An elegant roast rack of lamb needn't be a meal reserved for a fine restaurant, as the ease of this recipe will attest. Young lamb is best served from medium-rare to medium-well.

FOR FOUR SERVINGS

2 frenched 8-bone lamb racks

2 teaspoons olive oil
2 tablespoons garlic,
  coarsely chopped
1 teaspoon chopped rosemary
1 teaspoon chopped thyme
1 teaspoon chopped marjoram
1 teaspoon chopped tarragon
¼ cup chopped Italian parsley
1 teaspoon lavender flowers*
½ teaspoon black pepper
2 tablespoons coarse sea salt
Use only edible flowers

PREHEAT OVEN TO 425°

SPECIAL EQUIPMENT NEEDED

10 inch cast iron or ovenproof pan

Coat the lamb with the olive oil. Rub the garlic into the scored cuts in the lamb fat. Mix the fresh herbs and the pepper. Pat a generous coating of herb mixture on the racks. Let them stand for two hours.

FOR THE VEGETABLES

3 cups eggplant, in 1 inch dice

2 cups zucchini, in ¾ inch dice

1 cup carrots, in ¾ inch dice

2 cups red onions, in 1 inch dice

12 peeled garlic cloves

2 tablespoons olive oil

1 teaspoon kosher salt

½ teaspoon black pepper

½ cup veal or beef stock

Toss the vegetables with the oil, salt and pepper.

Heat the skillet over medium-high heat. Place the racks, fat side down to cook until well seared, about 5 minutes. Turn them over and add the vegetables. Sprinkle the lamb with coarse salt and place the pan in the oven. Cook for 15 minutes, then reduce the temperature to 350°.

Cook the lamb to a thermometer-checked internal temperature of 120°, for medium-rare. Remove the lamb, cover with foil and hold. Continue roasting the vegetables until they are tender. Remove them to a serving platter and hold warm. Degrease the roasting pan. Add the stock and deglaze, reducing the volume by half.

Cut each rack in four pieces, serving two double-bone chops per person. Spoon jus over them and serve with the roasted vegetables.

ALTERNATE SERVING SUGGESTIONS

Serve steamed vegetables: baby green beans, broccoli, young carrots or asparagus. Serve with the celery root puree on page 65 or the French lentils on page 59.

If You Must Have Mint...

From England came the tradition of mint sauce served with lamb, or more precisely, mutton. The meat's strong flavor was enhanced and the odor was masked by this vinegar-based sauce. Stateside, we strayed from the true English sauce to the unexplained mint flavored apple jelly. If you must have mint with your lamb, try this adapted version of both styles.

MAKES ONE CUP

12 ounces mint jelly

⅔ cup white vinegar

2 cups chopped fresh mint

½ cup sugar

¼ cup creme de menthe

Simmer all the ingredients until it is reduced to 1 cup. Strain it and serve in a small pitcher.

Braised Lamb Shanks

Partly due to economics and partly because I adore braised meats in general, I discovered lamb shanks as a diversion from the pricey chops and racks. The succulent richness of slow cooked shank meat falling off the bone into a full bodied sauce of red wine, tomatoes and herbs never loses its appeal. When served over a creamy polenta I've saved an airline ticket to Florence.

SERVES SIX   PREHEAT OVEN TO 350°

EQUIPMENT NEEDED

Covered braising pot large
enough to hold the shanks

6 lamb shanks
2 tablespoons canola oil

1½ cups diced onion
1½ cups diced carrots
1½ cups diced celery
8 whole garlic cloves
3 tablespoons flour
2 cups diced, seeded, chopped
* plum tomatoes*
2 tablespoons tomato paste
2 cups veal stock
2 cups red wine, good Chianti,
Sangiovese or Montepulciano
4 sprigs fresh thyme
6 bay leaves
chopped zest of ½ orange
2 tablespoonds kosher salt
1 tablespoon black pepper
¼ cup currant jelly
2 tablespoons potato starch,
* dissolved in ¼ cup water*

chopped Italian parsley

Heat the oil in the heavy pot and carefully brown the shanks thoroughly over moderately high heat. Remove the meat and add the garlic, celery, onions and carrots. Cook while stirring until they color lightly. Add the flour and stir to mix it in. Add the tomatoes, thyme, bay, orange zest, stock, tomato paste and wine. Bring to a simmer and return the shanks to the pan. Season with the salt and pepper and place the covered pan in the oven to braise. Adjust the temperature to keep the liquid barely simmering. Check the meat after 2 hours. It is done when it almost falls off the bone when lifted out of the pan.

Carefully remove the shanks to a platter and keep warm. Discard the bay leaves and thyme sprigs. Skim the fat off the surface, add the currant jelly and potato starch. Simmer until the sauce is *slightly* thickened. Ladle the sauce over the shanks and garnish with chopped parsley.

Pan Grilled Peppered Venison With Balsamic Cherry Sauce

The heading of this recipe need not intimidate you. While the ingredients take some planning to gather, once assembled it is a very quick preparation. I'm including it because it has been a stand-out Ranch favorite for many years and just the suggestion of venison conjures exotic images of wild, open spaces.

Our source for venison is New Zealand where 'ranchers' line their property with eight foot fences and raise a breed of Red Deer highly esteemed for its lean and tender meat. There are mail order sources to purchase New Zealand Venison, see Sources.

I suggest buying a boneless, trimmed loin or tenderloin because it cooks quickly and carves easily. This cut of venison is best prepared rare to medium-rare [120°-125°] so it will remain juicy and tender. Serve this elegant main course with wild rice, page 56 and melted cabbage, page 82.

FOR EIGHT SERVINGS
3 pounds Venison Loin
1½ cups full-bodied red wine;
   a Zinfandel or Syrah
2 medium shallots, halved
2 sprigs fresh thyme
4 bay leaves

¼ cup peppercorn blend
   coarsely ground
1 teaspoon kosher salt
2 tablespoons canola oil

⅓ cup veal glace
⅓ cup dark cherry jam
¼ cup balsamic vinegar
⅓ cup dried tart cherries
½ teaspoon kosher salt
1 teaspoon potato starch dissolved in 1 tablespoon of water

Marinate the venison in the wine, shallots, thyme and bay leaves for 12 hours.
Remove the meat and pat dry. Reduce the marinade by one half over medium heat. Strain and reserve.
Rub the meat with salt and pepper. Brown the venison in an ovenproof pan then roast it to an internal temperature of 115°. Remove the venison and hold it warm. Deglaze the pan with the reduced marinade, adding the glace, jam, vinegar, salt, cherries and potato starch. Simmer to thicken slightly. Carve the venison thinly and serve the slices *over* the sauce on warmed plates.

Melted Cabbage

SERVES SIX - EIGHT

3 quarts *thinly* sliced Savoy or
Napa cabbage
¼ pound [1 stick] sweet butter
2 teaspoons kosher salt
½ teaspoon white pepper

Blanch the cabbage in a large pot of boiling water for 1 minute. Immediately refresh in very cold water to set the color. Drain well and spread the cabbage out on a towel to absorb excess water.

Melt the butter in a heavy sauce pan and add the cooked cabbage with the salt and pepper. Slowly cook for about 20 minutes over low heat until the cabbage 'melts' and absorbs all the butter. Serve immediately.

Balsamic Onions

This is a delicious side dish that compliments all varieties of meats and grilled foods. The sweet taste of caramelized onions is pleasantly balanced with the deep, rich flavor of Balsamic vinegar.

SERVES SIX

4 *large red onions, sliced*
¼ pound sweet butter
½ cup sugar
2 teaspoons kosher salt
½ teaspoon black pepper
1½ cups Balsamic vinegar

In a heavy-bottomed sauce pan over medium-low heat slowly cook the onions in the butter until they are lightly colored. Add the sugar, salt and pepper and continue cooking to dissolve the sugar. When the onions begin to stick to the pan add the vinegar and deglaze while stirring. Simmer 10 minutes and serve.

CHAPTER SIX

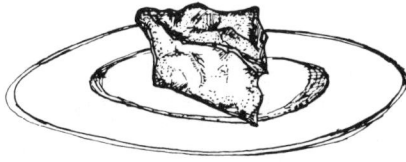

Desserts

and

Breads

Cookie's Biscuits

This recipe was burned into a sideboard of Cookie's chuckwagon, found in pieces after a terrible accident resulting from a very heated argument with the cowboys over Cookie's missing cat, Lucky.

MAKES ONE DOZEN

EQUIPMENT NEEDED
13" X 8" X 2" BAKING PAN

3½ cups unbleached flour
¼ cup sugar
4 tablespoons baking powder
2 teaspoons salt
⅔ cup shortening
1 cup buttermilk
¼ cup lowfat milk
3 eggs, beaten
4 tablespoons melted butter

PREHEAT OVEN TO 350°

Mix the eggs, buttermilk and milk. Blend the flour, shortening, sugar, salt and baking powder in a food processor. Remove to a bowl and add the egg mixture. Stir *just* until blended. Turn the dough onto the buttered and floured baking sheet and pat it to cover the sheet evenly. Score with a floured knife to mark the biscuits and bake for 20 - 25 minutes, or until golden brown. Brush with melted butter. Serve.

Chuckwagon Cornbread

EQUIPMENT NEEDED:
10" cast iron skillet

½ pound sweet butter, melted
3 beaten eggs
1 quart milk
5 cups organic stone ground
  yellow corn meal
3 cups unbleached all purpose
  flour
½ cup sugar
2 teaspoons salt
3 tablespoons baking powder

PREHEAT OVEN TO 375°

Beat the eggs, and milk together. Blend the corn meal, flour, baking powder, salt and sugar in a large bowl. Add the egg mixture and stir while adding 6 tablespoons of the melted butter.

Place the skillet in the oven with the remaining butter. When the butter begins to color pour in the batter and bake for about 20 minutes or until the center rises slightly and a toothpick inserted comes out clean.

ADDITIONS TO THE BATTER

½ cup sliced roasted green chiles
1 cup fresh cut corn

¼ cup dark chile powder
⅔ cup roasted pinenuts

A Bar A Ranch Hotcakes

Its not a bona fide ranch breakfast without a stack of these in front of you. Our Colorado grown organic flour blended with Stringtown Grocery eggs from Iowa make a batter that rises gracefully off the griddle in the fashion of a true hotcake. Use premium eggs and flour purchased at a health food store to duplicate our results.

MAKES ONE DOZEN PANCAKES

2 cups organic all purpose flour
2 tablespoons sugar
1 teaspoon kosher salt
1 teaspoon baking powder
½ teaspoon baking soda
2 cups buttermilk
2 eggs
¼ cup sweet butter, melted

canola oil for the griddle

PREHEAT GRIDDLE OR CAST IRON SKILLET

Mix the dry ingredients in a bowl. In another bowl beat the eggs and add the melted butter while whisking. Add the buttermilk and stir well. Add the dry mix to the egg mixture. Stir quickly until the batter is *just* blended. If the batter appears too thick after resting - add some milk to thin it. Lightly oil the griddle or pan with a paper towel. A splash of water sent dancing immediately signals the right temperature. Pour or spoon batter to make 6 inch pancakes. They are ready to flip when the edges bubble and they are brown underneath. Flip them and let them bake untouched. Resist the temptation to pat them with the spatula, these are *cakes* and they are meant to be light. Let them rise fully and serve immediately.

Banana Pecan Pancakes

Puree ripe bananas to make 1 cup. Substitute the puree for 1 cup of the buttermilk in the preceeding recipe and omit the sugar. Add 1 cup of toasted pecan pieces to the batter.

Summer Berry Pancakes

When the batter is on the griddle sprinkle raspberries, blueberries or blackberries onto the pancakes. Flip the cakes and cook as usual.

Railroad French Toast

This is an updated version of a classic served in the dining cars of the old Santa Fe Railroad when they still had passenger trains. I prefer to use a hearty country French bread with a good crust, sliced thick and slowly cooked in butter.

SERVES SIX

PREHEAT HEAVY SKILLET

12 *thick slices of rustic style French bread*

8 *large eggs, beaten*

3 *tablespoons sugar*

1½ *cups milk*

¾ *cup heavy cream*

1 *teaspoon cinnamon*

2 *tablespoons vanilla extract*

3 *cups crushed corn flakes*

¼ *cup sweet butter [1 stick]*

Vermont maple syrup

Beat the eggs with the sugar and cinnamon. Add the cream, milk and vanilla. Dip the bread into the batter just long enough to coat both sides. Dredge the battered bread in the cornflakes, pat gently and place the slices into the skillet with some of the butter. Repeat with enough pieces to fill pan. Cook over moderate heat until golden brown. Turn and cook other side. Hold cooked toasts in a warm oven as you finish cooking all the slices. Serve with pure maple syrup.

Butterscotch Apple Compote

Decadently rich, this fruit sauce can launch basic pancakes, waffles, crêpes and French toast into the realm of dessert.

SERVES SIX

4 *Granny Smith apples, peeled, cored and thickly sliced*

¼ *cup sweet butter*

½ *cup brown sugar*

½ *cup sugar*

2 *cups heavy cream*

In a heavy sauce pan cook the apple slices in the butter, stirring minimally until the apples begin to color. Add the sugars and shake the pan to dissolve. Cook over moderate heat until the butter and sugars turn to a caramel color. Off the heat add the cream. Careful, it may spatter and pop. Return to heat to dissolve the caramel in the cream. Simmer 10 minutes until thickened. Serve warm.

Crème Brulée

This very popular dessert is made from a versatile custard used in Crème Caramel and Pots de Crème; three French desserts that easily make the transition to cowboy country. This cool and creamy change of pace with a crunchy sugar crust is traditionally vanilla, but many other flavors can be made from the same base.

MAKES SIX SERVINGS OF FIVE OUNCES EACH

PREHEAT OVEN TO 325°

6 *six ounce ceramic baking cups*

SPECIAL EQUIPMENT NEEDED: BAKING PAN WITH 2" SIDES LARGE ENOUGH TO HOLD THE CUPS

PORTABLE PROPANE TORCH

3 cups heavy cream
1 cup half and half
12 egg yolks
¾ cup sugar
1 vanilla bean
superfine granulated sugar

Whisk the yolks and sugar together until light colored. Scald the cream, half and half and vanilla bean mixture. Slowly pour it into the egg mixture while stirring gently. **Try not to create bubbles or foam.**

Remove the vanilla bean. Strain the mixture through a fine sieve into the baking cups, filling them to ½ inch from the top. Place the dishes in the pan and fill it with boiling water to a level halfway up the dishes. Loosely cover the pan with aluminum foil and place it into the oven, careful not to splash water into cups.

Cook until the center of the custards appear lightly set when gently shaken, about 25 minutes.

The cooling period is important. The custards need to settle and chill over a 4 hour period. Cool them at room temperature for one hour before putting them in the refrigerator lightly covered. When fully chilled the custard will set to a very thick creamy consistency under the firmer surface layer.

Before serving sprinkle about a tablespoon of sugar on the custard and caramelize it with a hand held propane torch or under a very hot broiler. Keep the torch 3-4 inches from the sugar and move it constantly. The sugar will cook VERY quickly. When it is bubbling and brown it is done. Cool five minutes before serving.

Black and White Brownies

A popular combination of two famous favorites, fudgy chocolate and creamy cheesecake.

MAKES TWO DOZEN

EQUIPMENT NEEDED
9" X 11" X 1" BAKING SHEET

2 tablespoons cool,melted butter
5 ounces semisweet chocolate
2 ounces unsweetened chocolate
7 ounces soft unsalted butter
1¼ cups extrafine sugar
3 eggs
¾ cup flour
pinch of Kosher salt

1¼ pounds cream cheese
¾ cup extrafine sugar
2 eggs
1 teaspoon pure vanilla

PREHEAT OVEN TO 325°

Generously butter the baking pan. Break up the chocolates into pieces and melt in a small bowl set over hot water.

Beat the sugar and the soft butter until light. Incorporate the three eggs, one at a time. Add the cooled, melted chocolates and blend. Fold in the flour and the salt. Set aside.

Beat the cream cheese and the ¾ cup sugar until smooth. Beat in two eggs, one at a time. Add the vanilla and mixwell. Spread half of the chocolate mixture in the baking pan, then cover with the cheese mixture.

Drop spoonfuls of the remaining chocolate mixture over the cheese and 'marbleize' by quickly swirling with a spoon in circular motions. Bake for 45 minutes to 1 hour. Test with a small knife inserted in the center. It should come out slightly moist, not dry. Let the pan cool for 1 hour before cutting the brownies.

Big Creek Brownies

After a sometimes gentle, sometimes rowdy ride your horse reaches the calm and shady bend in the stream called Big Creek. The smoke of the lunchtime fires sifts through the willows on a gentle breeze and a cold lemonade sweetly rinses the last of the dust off your tongue. How that magic air mixes with campfire food to make the memory... and let's just grab another brownie before we head on home...

MAKES TWO DOZEN

EQUIPMENT NEEDED

9" x 11"x 2" baking pan

2 tablespoons melted butter, cooled

4 ounces unsweetened chocolate

½ pound butter

2 cups sugar

1 teaspoon vanilla

4 eggs

1 cup all purpose flour

pinch kosher salt

4 ounces walnuts [optional]

PREHEAT OVEN TO 350

Butter the baking pan with 2 tablespoons melted butter. Melt the chocolate with ½ pound butter in a bowl set over boiling water. Add the sugar and vanilla and blend well. Beat in the eggs, adding one at a time as each gets incorporated. Gently fold in the flour with the salt and then the nuts. Turn the batter into the pan and bake for 20-25 minutes. Test with the point of a small knife inserted into the center. The brownies are done when the knife comes out dry. The brownies need to cool at least 30 minutes before cutting them.

Cream Scones with Ginger and Currants

A Bar A Ranch Pastry chef Janet Dresser brought these from her home in San Francisco long before their popularity traveled East. Once Bob Howe latched onto them as a regular bakery inspection confiscation, they found a loving home with our guests and our staff. Homemade jam never tasted so good.

MAKES EIGHT LARGE SCONES
EQUIPMENT NEEDED
10" x 14" baking sheet

1½ cups cake flour
1½ cups all purpose flour
¼ cup sugar
2 large eggs
5 tablespoons sweet butter
1 tablespoon baking powder
¾ cup heavy cream
4 tablespoons chopped crystallized ginger
½ cup currants
½ teaspoon sea salt

PREHEAT OVEN TO 350°

Blend the flours, baking powder, sugar and salt. Cut the butter into small pieces and cut it into the flour mixture with a pastry blender or food processor until it resembles corn meal. Beat the eggs and add them to the cream. Stir in the currants and the ginger. Pour the egg mixture into the flour mixture and quickly stir *just* to moisten evenly. **Don't overmix.** Turn the dough onto a lightly floured board. Form into a flattened 10 inch round. Cut into 8 wedges and place the scones onto a lightly buttered baking sheet. Bake until they are lightly browned, about 20 minutes. Cool on rack.

POSSIBLE ADDITIONS TO THE DOUGH

dried cranberries
toasted almonds
candied orange peel
dried cherries

chocolate chips
chopped dates
dried strawberries
candied lemon peel

Vanilla Rice Pudding with Ginger-Cardamom Syrup

A traditional comfort dessert takes on an exotic flair with pungent Tahitian vanilla, Indian spices and Australian crystallized ginger. Arborio rice makes this version exceptionally rich and creamy.

MAKES SIX-EIGHT SERVINGS

FOR THE SYRUP
2 cups water
1 cup sugar
¾ teaspoon decorticated
   cardamon seeds
8 slices ginger [¾ inch round]

Dissolve the sugar in the water over low heat. Add the cardamon and fresh ginger slices. Simmer gently until reduced by half. Set aside to cool. Strain.

FOR THE PUDDING
5 cups lowfat milk
1 Tahitian vanilla bean, split
4 inch cinnamon stick
1 cup arborio rice
2 tablespoons chopped
   crystallized ginger
pinch sea salt

In a heavy bottomed non-aluminum saucepan bring the milk, vanilla, crystallized ginger, cinnamon and salt to a simmer. Add the rice and cook slowly while stirring for 30 minutes. Add the sugar and simmer for 15 minutes more, until the rice is very soft.

½ cup sugar
2 egg yolks
½ cup heavy cream

In a small bowl mix the yolks with the cream. Stir this mixture into the simmering pudding. When it returns to a simmer, take it off the heat. Remove the vanilla bean and cinnamon. Let cool and serve in small cups drizzled with the syrup.

The world's finest crystallized ginger comes from the land down under. Searching out the select Australian ginger is well worth the extra effort.

Chocolate Eclairs

It seems these chocolate eclairs have been a regular feature at the A Bar A for generations. Perhaps they got their start in the 50's when the ranch kitchen was staffed by European chefs. When we serve them somebody always shares a story about the early days.

MAKES ONE DOZEN   PREHEAT OVEN TO 400°

EQUIPMENT NEEDED
11" x 14" baking sheet
1 tablespoon butter
Pastry bag with ½ inch round tip

PATE A CHOUX
1 cup water
¼ pound sweet butter [1 stick]
pinch sea salt
1 cup all purpose flour
4 large beaten eggs

Butter the baking sheet generously. Bring the water, butter and salt to a simmer in a small saucepan. The butter should be completely melted when the water boils. Off the heat add all the flour at once and stir it vigorously to make a smooth dough. Stir over the heat for 30 seconds to dry the dough. Again off heat, beat in half the eggs with a wooden spoon. When completely absorbed, beat in the remaining eggs. Put the dough in a pastry bag with a plain ½ inch round tip. Squeeze out twelve 4 inch lines of dough onto a lightly buttered baking sheet. Leave a space of two inches between them. Bake for 20 minutes, then reduce heat to 325° for 20 minutes more or until they are evenly browned and dry inside. Remove to cool on a rack.

PASTRY CREAM
4 cups milk
6 egg yolks
1 cup sugar
1 teaspoon pure vanilla
⅓ cup flour
⅓ cup corn starch

3 tablespoons butter

Beat the yolks with the sugar. Add ½ cup of the milk, the flour and the cornstarch. Beat well to make a **smooth** mixture. Put the remaining milk and vanilla in a non-aluminum saucepan to boil. Pour the milk slowly into the eggs while beating with a whisk. Return the mixture to the pan and cook while stirring until it boils for two minutes. Put the cream in a bowl, coat the surface with butter, cover and chill.

EQUIPMENT NEEDED
Pastry bag with small star tip

Place cooled cream in a pastry bag fitted with the small star tip. Using the tip like a drill make a hole in the bottom of each eclair and fill them with cream through the hole.

Boil the heavy cream and add the chocolate, broken in pieces. Let it stand 10 minutes to melt. Stir well to blend smoothly. When it cools to room temperature frost each eclair. Refrigerate the eclairs before serving.

GANACHE GLAZE
5 ounces semi-sweet chocolate
½ cup heavy cream

Key Lime Pie

MAKES ONE 9 INCH PIE

PREHEAT OVEN TO 300°

EQUIPMENT NEEDED
9 inch deep dish pie pan

2 cups graham cracker crumbs
4 tablespoons melted butter

*14 ounce can sweetened
  condensed milk*
*½ cup Nellie & Joe's Key Lime
  juice [see Sources]*
3 egg yolks
⅛ ounce powdered gelatin
2 tablespoons water
1½ cups heavy cream, whipped

Blend the cracker crumbs with the melted butter in a food processor. Pack them evenly into the pie pan to form a crust. Bake in the oven for 15 minutes to brown and set.

Sprinkle the gelatin into the water to soften. In a small stainless bowl blend the milk, egg yolks and softened gelatin. Place the bowl over a pot of **simmering** water and cook for 5 minutes, while beating **continuously**. Don't overcook the mixture or the eggs will scramble. Set aside to cool. Stir in the lime juice and chill until it softly sets. Beat the cream to stiff peaks and fold it into the filling. Pour the filling into the pie pan and refrigerate at least 12 hours before cutting and serving.

Pecan Bars

Whenever Janet, our pastry chef, made these chewy treats she'd leave a couple on my desk to make sure I got one. She knew well that if she didn't, I wouldn't get a second chance.

MAKES EIGHTEEN BARS
EQUIPMENT NEEDED

10"x 15"x 1" baking sheet
aluminum foil

½ pound butter [2 sticks]
½ cup superfine sugar
1 large egg
¼ teaspoon sea salt
grated rind of 1 lemon
3 cups all purpose flour

PREHEAT OVEN TO 375°

Line the baking sheet with aluminum foil. Butter the foil then refrigerate the pan while making the crust.

FOR THE CRUST

Cream the butter and the sugar until light. Blend in the lemon peel, salt and egg. Add the flour and mix to form the crumbly dough. Carefully pat the dough out *evenly* onto the foiled pan and prick holes overall with the tines of a fork. Refrigerate for 30 minutes. Bake for 20 minutes, popping any large bubbles that form during the baking. Remove to cool.

FOR THE TOPPING

½ pound butter [2 sticks]
½ cup honey
¼ cup sugar
1⅛ cup dark brown sugar
¼ cup heavy cream
5 cups pecan halves and pieces

Cook the butter with the honey to melt completely. Add the sugars and stir to dissolve. Then let the mixture boil undisturbed for 2 minutes. Stir in the cream and the pecans. With a slotted spoon, sprinkle the nuts evenly over the baked crust. Drizzle the sauce over the pecans, filling all the gaps. Return to the oven to bake for 25 minutes. Remove and cool before unmolding and cutting.

TO UNMOLD THE BARS

Once cooled, place a second baking sheet on top of the pecan bars and flip to invert. Remove the foil and flip back over into the unlined pan. Cut the bars with a sharp knife and serve.

Deb's Awesome Datenut Bars

This wonderful recipe came to me from a friend and a fellow date lover, Debbie Maddox, who warmed our hearts and tummies at the Terrace Restaurant on cold Breckenridge 'parade days' with platefuls of her irresistable datenut bars.

EQUIPMENT NEEDED
12"X 7"X 1" BAKING PAN

MAKES 12 BARS

20 *Medjool dates*
1 *cup water*
¾ *cup honey*

1 *teaspoon vanilla*
1 *tablespoon lemon juice*

1½ *cups whole wheat flour*
1½ *cups rolled oats*
½ *teaspoon salt*
1 *teaspoon baking powder*

¾ *cup unsweetened coconut,*
  shredded
½ *cup finely chopped pecans*
½ *cup finely chopped almonds*
¾ *cup melted sweet butter*

PREHEAT OVEN TO 400°

Remove the pits from the dates and cook them with the water and the honey until very thick. Remove from the heat and add the vanilla and the lemon juice. Set aside to cool completely.

Mix together the flour, salt, oats and baking powder. Add the coconut, pecans and almonds. Stir in the melted butter and mix well. Pat ⅔ of the mixture into the bottom of the baking pan. Pour the date mixture over it and sprinkle the remaining mixture over the top. Put the bars into the oven and immediately reduce the temperature to 300°. Bake until the topping is lightly browned, about one hour. Cut the bars while they are still warm.

Glossary

ACHIOTE   A Mexican condiment that is sold in the form of a dense paste. Its principal ingredient is ground annatto beans. Most Yucateco families have their own family recipe, much like Garam Masala and curry in India. A commercial version is available from good Mexican and Latin American grocers.

BLANCH   Cooking food in a quantity of boiling water. This term pertains to both parcooking as well as complete cooking.

BOUQUET GARNI   The French term for a bundle of aromatics and herbs used in stews, sautés and soups. It consists of short stalks of celery encasing sprigs of thyme, parsley and bay leaves. It is tied tightly with cotton string and removed when the cooking is done. I indicate bouquet garnies of different lengths as a form of measure.

BRAISE   Food cooked in a liquid, in a sealed recipient for an extended period. This method cooks slowly while tenderizing and blending flavors.

BRUNOISE   A term taken from the French which describes a food cut into a *very fine* dice. Mostly seen used with aromatics like peppers, celery, carrots and onions. Difficult to master, the technique demonstrates expert control of the knife.

BUTTER   Butter is available in salted and unsalted form. I suggest always cooking with unsalted butter so you know how much salt you are adding to the food. While all butter is the product of the same source, it varies widely in taste, texture and price.

The taste is a direct result of the cows' diet and the treatment of the cream. Most butter is produced by huge corporate dairies, and some are clearly better than others. If you are fortunate to have access to a smaller regional or even local dairy, you might try theirs. A component of nearly all butter is water. More specifically it is a milk-solid solution that the Department of Agriculture allows butter to contain at a regulated maximum percentage of 20%. The more water, the poorer the value, and indeed the poorer the quality. Water in butter causes more problems in baking fine pastry doughs and cakes, than in other cooking. In a hot pan, however, the water that is found in butter can spatter dangerously.

Usually the price you pay reflects the amount of water present, because it costs more to remove it. There are French butters available that contain less than most American ones. The cost is considerably higher. I suggest if you like butter and you use it carefully, try the French, or an American product from Egg Farm Dairy [see Sources]. There's no doubt that when butter is an important component in a recipe, there's no substitute for the finest quality.

Clarified butter   Clarified butter is the result of removing the water and milk solids through slow cooking. To clarify butter cook it over medium-low heat until foam appears on the surface. Care-fully remove it. Continue cooking until the solid particles can be seen at the bottom of the pan. Don't cook at a temperature that boils the water at the bottom of the pot. The butter will actually appear clear with the water and milk solids segregated neatly on the bottom of the pot. This should take about 20 minutes. Carefully pour off the butter leaving the water in the pot.

CARDAMOM, Green pods   Seeds of a tropical plant which are about the size of coarse salt . They are dark in color and very pungent in aroma and flavor. They can be purchased in their pods, called whole cardomon or removed, called decorticated. Cardomon is available ground but it loses its freshness quickly once ground.

CHERVIL   A very delicate herb which looks like a lacy version of parsley. Chervil is very perishable and its use is as a fresh herb only. It has a very mild anise-like flavor. It is a hardy grower for the home gardener.

CHINOIS   A cone shaped strainer available in varying mesh sizes depending on the desired result. Commonly used for passing sauces and creams. The name describes the shape of a Chinese hat.

CHIPOTLE PEPPERS   Chipotle peppers are dried, smoked ripe Jalapeño peppers. They usually are considerably hotter than their fresh counterparts. Their flavor is unique and unmistakable. When used for sauces or salsas, it helps to soften them in warm water, then the seeds and stem can easily be removed. A quality chipotle pepper in Adobo is widely available in cans at specialty markets.

CILANTRO, Coriander Leaf, Mexican Parsley   An herb that is very distinctive in taste. Widely used in Asian, Mexican and Indian cooking, cilantro is an indispensable ingredient in fresh salsas and many Oriental dishes, particularly Vietnamese and Thai cuisines.

DEEP FRYING   As Americans, we consume large quantities of fried foods. However, almost none of us prepares them in our kitchens. The ability to deep fry in the home kitchen can expand the menu possibilities and present some challenges at the same time. It can be a healthier way to eat fried foods if good quality oil is used. Use the healthiest frying oil you can afford-canola or safflower work well. Unrefined oils are easier to digest and can have better nutritional content than hydrogenated oils that are denatured during the refining. Small portable fryers are available but their size is generally too small for easy preparation of anything in quantity. I suggest an inexpensive, even second-hand pot with a lid. One with 10 quart capacity is good. With a simple wire frying basket and a frying thermometer you are ready.

When you are done frying, let the pot cool, replace the lid and store it safely where it can't be spilled. Next time you fry, you are ready. The frying oil is easily cleaned by straining it when it is warm, not hot, through a paper coffee filter. The oil should be strained when sediment becomes noticeable and stored in a cool place. The oil can be used for up to 6 weeks or when it looks like weak coffee, whichever comes first. Always discard your oil in a sealed container in the trash, never down the drain.

DEGLAZE   The removal of cooked-on food juices from pans by the addition of a liquid: stock, wine, water, cream etc. Simmering while scraping is sometimes necessary.

DEGREASE   Removal of fat that rises to the surface of a soup, stock or sauce. Most easily done with a ladle; be careful not to remove too much of the liquid under the fat.

DESCUM   Removal of a film of foam or cooked particles which rise to the surface of cooking food. Often found at the beginning of cooking beans or stocks when the foods throw off impurities as they come to a boil.

DICE   To cut foods into small square shaped pieces, usually between ⅛ inch and ½ inch. To easily arrive at uniformly sized pieces first cut the item into strips the width of the dice, then turn the strips and cut them into the same size squares.

DREDGE   To lightly coat a food in a dry powder, flour or crumb. Sometimes the food is first coated in beaten egg to help form a crust that will stay on the food during cooking.

DRIED FRUITS   Many more fruits are being dried for use in our cooking. In addition to apricots, prunes and dates, we can now find cherries, both sweet and sour, strawberries, blueberries, kiwifruit, bananas, pineapple and cranberries. Most are easily found at a specialty grocer or good health food stores. Always look to cook with interesting textures and concentrated flavors. Dried fruits can serve that purpose.

EGG WHITES   The white of the egg is low in cholesterol and indispensible in all facets of cooking. They store well frozen, therefore always save them from recipes that call for yolks only.
Beating Egg Whites   To beat egg whites well they need to be free of any yolk, grease or water. The best way is in an unlined copper bowl, which has been cleaned with vinegar and a pinch of salt. With copper a chemical reaction occurs which stabilizes the whites holding them full and stiff. For cooks using a KitchenAid mixer, copper bowl inserts are available through Williams-Sonoma and the Chef's Catalog. [see Sources] When beating egg whites in stainless, glass or ceramic bowls, add a pinch of cream of tartar to provide the stabilizing acid. Don't beat them too long,or they can become dry and grainy, making them difficult to fold in.
FOLD   A manner of mixing to incorporate ingredients gently. Using a rubber spatula or wooden spoon the ingredients underneath are lifted to the top of the mixture. Use repetitive motions while turning the bowl.

GARLIC   A member of the Alium, or onion family, garlic is a very popular ingredient. It is used around the world in cuisines from Mexico to the Orient. It is used both raw and cooked. There are a few varieties of garlic sold commercially. The white skinned variety is milder than its purple skinned relative, while large 'elephant' garlic is the mildest of all. A *head* of garlic is composed of many *cloves*.
To skin garlic   Gently crush whole cloves under a heavy knife or dropped in boiling water for 3 minutes, they peel easily.
To roast garlic   Cut the top off the head of garlic, about ½inch. Brush lightly with olive oil and roast in a 325° oven for about 45 minutes. Cover with foil and roast 20 minutes more. When cooked the garlic can be squeezed out of the cloves through the open top.

GINGER ROOT   A fresh underground root cultivated for its culinary and medicinal uses. Ginger has a light brown papery skin that is peeled off before use. Choose firm, plump roots with smooth skin. Chop it finely for use in all Asian cooking including Indian cuisine.
Crystalized Ginger   Slow cooked in sugar syrup, ginger becomes candied and sweet.

GLACE   A glace is the reduction of a stock by slow simmering. As the water evaporates the stock becomes concentrated. The stock also throws off impurities and fat while it cooks. Remove these by-products with a spoon to ensure a mostly clean, powerful version of the original stock. Storage is much easier since the volume is reduced so much.

Depending on the natural gelatin content, when cold the glace becomes syrupy or gelled hard. Add water to make any desired strength. Often made from veal, this product can be found at 'gourmet' grocery and specialty stores. Meat and poultry glaces can be stored for weeks in your refrigerator or for months in the freezer.

HERBS   [also see specific herb] I recommend buying dried herbs in small quantities as they can quickly lose their flavor. Try to find a health food store that buys in bulk so you can sniff before buying and purchase only what you'll use in a few weeks. Often grocery store stocks have been on the shelf for a long time.

Remember the finer the grind the stronger the flavor by volume and the faster they fade. Be aware that some irradiated products are making their way into the marketplace. These are herbs that pass through a light dose of radiation allegedly to increase shelf life. I choose to avoid them. Some herbs lose their flavor completely when dried so don't bother with dried chervil, parsley or cilantro.

Fresh herbs are now easily found in grocery stores. They are not inexpensive so choose carefully for freshness and buy only what you'll use in a couple days. They should be kept with their stems in a little water in the refrigerator. Wrap loosely with plastic to help them hold moisture. Fresh herbs stored in closed bags are fine until they start to spoil. Then they go fast. Always wash fresh herbs before using. If they are to be chopped, dry them well before chopping and always use a very sharp knife.

KITCHEN EQUIPMENT   Books have been written on the subject of equipment for the home kitchen. Tempted by all the catalogs we receive, our kitchens could be packed with every gadget and device imaginable. The new 'in' cookware color changes as often as our Presidents. It's easy to fall prey to the mentality that more is better, when it isn't. America's dream kitchens are looking like stark hotel kitchens with monster ranges and stainless steel refrigerators... all this when we are eating fewer meals at home than at any time in our history.

Very successful cooking can be accomplished with carefully chosen equipment designed and built for the long haul. Quality is more important than quantity and less is often better than more. As new appliances replace older ones we tend to collect redundant counter-clutter and soon we have nine things that blend. It's the

American way, and it keeps us in garage sales. Try to keep it simple. There are a few important areas that deserve mention here.

I am often asked what cookware is best. I am biased from my experience in France. I am seriously attached to copper as the best choice. The virtues of copper are numerous. They last forever, literally, as antique stores attest. Copper pots cook incredibly evenly. They never warp, bend or discolor food. They even clean up like non-stick pans. Today's copper cookware is available with stainless interiors to address the concern of the tin lining, which needs periodic replacement. They are not without their disadvantages. Copper requires some maintenance to look its best, if that is important to you. They are very heavy, even when empty, which is the reason they cook well. Copper satisfies the concerns of serious cooks; they are an investment in first class tools.

My second choice is cast iron, both with and without enamel finish. They share copper's virtues of even heating, durability and no taste transfer in the case of the enameled ones.

I'm not a huge fan of aluminum cookware. However when bonded to more durable metals, they are passable. Use pots with heavy bottoms and thick walls because aluminum pots tend to bottom-warp. Exercise caution when using metal utensils on aluminum because it scrapes off and can discolor some foods. There is ongoing research investigating the suspected link between aluminum ingestion and degenerative disease.

I've never found all-stainless cookware satisfactory. Stainless steel is a very quick and direct conductor of stove heat. Therefore, only use pans with thick bottoms. This helps to diffuse the heat, reducing the scorching and burning associated with stainless cookware. Stainless pans are very difficult to clean and they often develop 'hot spots'--places where foods regularly burn or stick. Only choose stainless pans when made in conjunction with other metals.

I am convinced that the oldest technologies are still the best choice...wood, copper and iron will always have a principal role in kitchens, their usefulness has stood the test of time.

Cutlery is an important consideration if owning and maintaining good tools is something that you feel strongly about. High quality knives are expensive and they require maintenance and sharpening. Knives are easier to use and safest when sharp. Buy only knives that you will actually need. Four or five different knives should be sufficient for most tasks. Specialty knives are helpful when you are doing any fish fileting, meat cutting, boning, carving etc.

I highly recommend investing in a a food processor. They make very short work of many kitchen tasks. It is important that the blade stay sharp to ensure even chopping and quick pureeing.

If you will be doing heavy mixing or bread making a KitchenAid mixer can be indispensable. But it makes a very large counter ornament if it is left unused. The attachments can eliminate other kitchen machines.

Wood just can't be replaced as a cutting surface. Plastics have tried to permanently retire wood, but they damage easily, stain, warp and are potentially more friendly towards dangerous bacteria. A regular mild bleaching keeps wood safe and long lived.

MARINATE   The process of soaking a food in a highly seasoned liquid or oil blend which can tenderize, impart flavor, color or even 'cook' a food without the use of heat.

OIL, COOKING   Always the subject of dietary discussions, oils used in our foods make up an important part of our diet. Only the finest quality should be considered. Culinary oils are derived from seeds, nuts and fruits. The oil is extracted either mechanically or chemically. Avoid those produced for the mass market by a refining process which uses a petroleum-based relative of gasoline, called benzine. Select instead those which are cold pressed or expeller extracted.

These include canola, safflower and sunflower which have a light taste and are for general use. Special purpose oils include those with distinctive flavors, like peanut, sesame, avocado, walnut and olive.

Olive oil is produced in several countries. Each region has its own distinctive style and taste. There is a range of flavors from powerful to mild. There are uses for each kind. Like wine, a good olive oil is one that you like, regardless of price. Extra virgin is considered the purest. It is a product of the first cold pressing. Subsequent pressings of the skins and pits produce an inferior oil, often used for blending. Strong flavored olive oils are used sparingly, as a seasoning. I recommend using a clean-tasting, mild version for everyday use.

The health benefits have just recently been recognized by the American medical establishment. Other countries have known this for centuries.

PEPPERS   Peppers of all kinds are used in cooking around the world. They are indispensable for adding color and flavor to foods and in some cases spicy heat to varying degrees. Many peppers contain Capsaicin, the component responsible for heat on our palate.

Hot peppers, often called chiles are heat-rated on the Scovill scale. The hottest chile is the Red Savina, a variety of Habañero rated at 500,000 units. The Jalapeno rates at a mere 50,000 units.

Peppers are eaten raw, cooked, pickled and dried. Dried peppers are ground for chili powders, including paprika.

Roasting and Peeling Peppers   When a recipe calls for roasted and peeled peppers there are two ways to do this. The peppers can be placed in direct contact with a flame to burn and blister the skin or they can be deep fried in oil until the skin blisters. In either case the peppers are then placed in a bowl and tightly covered to allow the steam to soften the skin. After 30 minutes the skin is easily removed. The peppers can then be seeded and used as needed.

PEPITAS   The Mexican name for pumpkin seeds, these long, green seeds can be found in ethnic markets or in health food stores. They sometimes are roasted and seasoned, but most often you'll find them raw. While easily toasted in the oven, take great care when frying because they pop violently and can end up all over your kitchen.

Classic Mexican recipes use pepitas extensively and therefore they have found their way into American Southwestern cuisine. They are great in stuffings, salads and sprinkled as garnish on foods of many kinds.

PINENUT   The small fruit of the piñonpine harvested from the cones. The nut has a thin, brittle shell that is difficult to remove. The process is expensive and therefore they are among the priciest nuts.

POBLANO PEPPER   Poblanos are used predominantly in Mexican cooking. They are very dark green, almost black, when best with a wide top and short body. Their flesh is thick and durable. The poblano is the choice for stuffing, as with Chiles Rellenos. While not considered hot, some recent varieties are being found to be quite spicy. In their dried form poblanos are known as Anchos. They are available at Mexican or Latin American markets.

RICE   Many different types of rice should be in any well stocked pantry. Choose a long grain white variety for the majority of your needs. Good quality rice comes from many places in the world. I suggest Basmati from Thailand or India, or a Texmati blend from the U.S. There are Japanese varieties and many from the Far East.

One of the finest is the Italian Arborio which comes in different grades. It is the only choice for risotto and puddings. Brown varieties cover a wide spectrum of nutty flavors, textures and grain size. Wild rice, not a true rice at all [it is a type of grass] is always popular. When buying wild rice always look for long, unbroken grains. The finest is grown in Canada and the northern Great Lakes region. Some is being produced in California, but it is inferior to the northern varieties.

I suggest buying the rice you use most often in large quantities: at least 5 or 10 lbs at a time. Rice uses different amounts of water in the cooking. It might take a couple tries to perfect the exact amount. Therefore if you buy in quantity you will need less experiments.

Also stay with a particular brand if you find one that you like. Basmati rice is a scented variety that is aged. It actually improves with age so you'll benefit from having it around for awhile.

SALT   Culinary salt somes in several forms and from different sources. The best all purpose salt is Kosher salt. It has few additives and its texture makes it very easy to hold between your fingers. I find having salt readily available in an open top container makes using it easier. Commercial granulated salt should be ignored. It has an adulterated taste due to its additives. Use a good quality granulated evaporated sea salt for your shakers. Coarse sea salt crystals are invaluable to any serious cook. Its flavor is clean and fresh. Once you enjoy the crunch of good salt on a steak, you'll never settle for bland table salt.

SAUTE   From the French meaning to jump, this term describes a cooking technique that uses high heat and a short cooking time. The food jumps in the pan while cooking. In classical terms it describes a family of longer- cooked dishes made with a variety of meats and sauces. The meat is first browned then cooked slowly in a liquid. Coq au Vin and Boeuf a la Bourguignonne are examples of sautés.

SERRANO CHILE   A small elongated pepper usually 2-3 inches in length and either green or red, depending on ripeness. Serranos are quite hot and their particular taste is highly perfumed. Caution with serranos and their seeds as they can be very hot.

SIMMER   This is a term found often in the recipes. The precise definition comes from the word 'shiver', which means the liquid is barely boiling. In practice we employ a broader use. When I specify simmer it means to cook at a **very** gentle boil, best described: a bubble here and a bubble there.

SOY SAUCE OR SHOYU   Shoyu or soy sauce is the result of fermenting soy beans. It is found in several different strengths and a variety of flavors. Choose carefully as some major brands are deceptive in their descriptions. Look for added colorants and preservatives and avoid them. In some recipes soy replaces some or all of the necessary salt.

STOCKS   The importance of stocks in the kitchen repertoire can not be overstated. They serve many purposes. While they are the backbone of soups and sauces, their most important role is their utilisation of 'scraps' created during kitchen work that otherwise might be thrown away. Many cast-offs are then used to fullest measure which not only enhances our food, but saves money. Once you understand how to incorporate stock-making into your kitchen routine, menu planning, shopping and cooking will come together as a family.

Making stocks changes the choices you make at the market. Using chicken as an example we can see this easily. Boneless chicken is many times the cost of whole birds, even cut up fryers. Learning the technique of removing breast meat from a whole chicken is well worth the time. You will then have all the rest of the chicken to use in many ways. Stock or soup can be made from the bones and scraps. Nothing is wasted. Most stock is a creation of leftovers, but there are times when you'll want to buy the ingredients. Choose meaty bones. Necks and backs from poultry, beef, pork and veal all work well. Here are a few rules:

Don't mix different meats/bones in a stock. Certain meat flavors, like beef, pork or lamb will overpower the taste of others.

Always start a stock with cold water and always add cold water when more is needed. Starting with cold water allows the meats to 'leech' out impurities as they start to cook, so descum the stock when it is first put on to cook. To replace the volume lost during cooking, add cold water which causes the fat in the stock to rise to the surface where it is easily removed. This should be done each time water is added.

Simmer, don't boil a stock. Vigorous boiling causes a stock to become cloudy, which is caused by the homogenization of the fat with the liquid. Skimming a stock is healthful and important. A soup or sauce made with a fat-homogenized stock will always have a fat slick on it as the stock continually 'throws off' the absorbed fat.

Don't use salt and pepper Since stock is a base ingredient there's no need to season it. A stock should be 'neutral'. All the specific seasoning will be done when the stock is used.

Choose vegetables carefully Use certain vegetables only in moderate amounts to round out the stock's flavor. Too much of any will overpower. Vegetables to use include: All members of the onion family, carrots, celery and tomatoes. **Stay away from:** Cabbages, broccoli, turnips, peppers, parsnips. Avoid squashes [unless you are making a vegetable stock], potatoes and leafy greens. These vegetables tend to impart a strong flavor to neutral stock, interfering with the meat flavor.

Don't overcook a stock Most meat based stocks will capture the flavor in 6 - 8 hours. Fish and vegetable stocks are faster. This needs not be continuous cooking time.

Cool a stock quickly After straining the stock it is ready for immediate use or it can be reduced to concentrate the flavor [See GLACE] Before storing, stock needs to be chilled quickly. Place it in a metal recipient that is immersed in an ice water bath. Stir it frequently. When cool, it can be covered and stored in the refrigerator.

Basic Beef or Veal Stock

MAKES TWO QUARTS

PREHEAT OVEN TO 350°

4 pounds meaty bones,
  neck or shank
4 carrots, cut in chunks
2 onions, unpeeled, quartered
6 stalks celery, cut into 4 inch
  pieces
1 cup tomato sauce
12 parsley stems
6 bay leaves
4 sprigs thyme

4 quarts cold water

Place the bones, carrots, onions and celery into a roasting pan. Roast in the oven for one hour. Stir during the cooking to evenly brown. Remove the pan from the oven and place bones and vegetables in a large pot. Put 2 cups water in the pan and deglaze over medium heat, scraping the caramelized juices off the pan bottom. Add the glaze to the bones and cover with the remaining cold water. Add the tomato, bay leaves, thyme and parsley. Simmer for 6 - 8 hours, skimming off the excess fat and scum as it cooks. Add cold water as needed to keep bones covered. Strain and simmer, reducing its volume to 2 quarts.

Basic Chicken Stock

MAKES TWO QUARTS

2 pounds chicken backs
3 carrots, cut in chunks
1 large, unpeeled onion,
  quartered
2 stalks celery
small bunch parsley
3 tablespoons tomato paste
4 bay leaves
4 sprigs thyme
4 quarts cold water

Place all the ingredients into a large stockpot. Slowly heat to a simmer. Skim the surface after the impurities rise in the form of scum. Continue to simmer for 4 hours. Strain the stock and chill immediately. Once cold the fat will rise to the top and harden, then it can be discarded or used in cooking.

This is known as white chicken stock because the chicken is used raw. A brown chicken stock is made after roasting the chicken with the aromatic vegetables in a 350° oven for 45 minutes. Proceed with the recipe after roasting the ingredients.

To Make Glace from Stock

Meat stocks can be reduced to a form which stores easily and adds full, rich flavor when needed. They are the secret weapon in making sauces that pack a punch. These reductions are called glace, or glaze.

Once a stock has been strained and degreased it can be slowly cooked, or reduced until it becomes concentrated and almost syrupy. In this form they store in a small container and can be used in very small quantities to enrich soups, stews and sauces. They are often used as a sauce by themselves. They also can be returned to a lighter form simply by adding water.

SUPREME Boneless breast meat of poultry that has the skin left on and upper arm bone left attached.

THYME There are many different thymes available for use in cooking. It is a common perenial which grows close to the ground. Some of the varieties include lemon, orange or pineapple thyme. It is a prominent player in French cooking. Considered an important 'aromatic', thyme is used in bouquet garnis and is associated with many fish and poultry dishes.

TOMATOES An indispensable food that comes in many varieties. Look for true vine-ripe tomatoes meaning they were left on the plant until the sun ripened them. Grocery store tomatoes are as hard as baseballs when picked green. They go through a chlorine bath by the dumptruck load, not even getting bruised. Then they are shut in warehouses where ethylene gas is pumped in to 'ripen' them and they are coated with carnauba or parafin wax...yumm. OR you can buy organics or vine-ripened tomatoes. If it doesn't smell like a tomato, don't buy it. A ripe tomato is a work of nature's art. Often Italian plum tomatoes are a better choice at the market. They work fine in salads too.

TRUFFLE OIL Oil infused with the peelings of either French black truffles or Italian white truffles. This formidable flavoring ingredient is used in small quantities in dishes including truffles and in recipes where wild mushrooms are used.

VANILLA Vanilla is a very important ingredient found mainly in desserts. It is grown in few places in the world, always within 20° of the Equator. The best vanilla comes from Madagascar and Tahiti. Vanilla beans are the dried and cured pods of the vanilla orchid. Harvesting is a very tedious and involved process and therefore vanilla is expensive. It is sold as a liquid extract, powder or whole bean. Store split beans in sugar and the vanilla bean will flavor the sugar for use in recipes. Beware of the artificial version, much of which comes from Mexico, where ironically, vanilla cultivation originated.

ZEST The outermost layer of citrus skin: lemon, lime, orange etc. used in recipes in raw form or cooked. Only the colored part of the peel should be used because the white layer beneath is very bitter. The zest is grated or removed in strips and often it is blanched before using. When cooked in simple syrup zests become candied.

Sources

THE CHEF'S CATALOG
1-800-338-3232
Professional quality kitchen equipment

D'ARTAGNAN
399-419 St. Paul Avenue
Jersey City, New Jersey 07306
1-800-327-8246
French specialty foods,
foie gras, duck products

EGG FARM DAIRY
2, John Walsh Blvd.
Peekskill, New York 10566
914-734-7343
1-800-CREAMERY
E-Mail: info@creamery.com
Handmade butter and cheese

GAME SALES INTERNATIONAL
P.O. Box 5314
Loveland, Colorado 80538
1-800-729-2090
Exotic meats, hard to find products
Venison, game birds, foie gras

NELLIE & JOE'S
1-800-546-3743
Key Lime Juice and Products from Key West, Florida

WILLIAMS-SONOMA
1-800-541-2233
Kitchen equipment, tools, furnishings
Foods and Specialty items

Notes

ABOUT THE AUTHOR

Kent Trebilcox has been passionate about cooking from a very early age. He was first introduced to the art by his mother and his grandmother, who were both from Italy. They prepared many of the foods familiar to their homes in Europe and the Orient, where they spent much of their lives.

After considerable travel in Europe following high school in Denver, Colorado, Mr. Trebilcox enrolled at the prestigious Cordon Bleu Cooking School for training in classic French cooking. Concurrently he completed rigorous training at L'Ecole Hotellière de Paris to become one of the first Americans to achieve the CAP, the important French Certification for Cooking.

While living in Paris he worked as a private corporate caterer and he worked with his mentor, Pierre Siri of La Chamaille Restaurant, to whom he credits his development as a chef.

After returning to the United States, Mr. Trebilcox held positions at many restaurants and taught and consulted on many projects. As the Executive Chef for the State of Colorado and Governor Richard D. Lamm, Mr. Trebilcox served Heads of State, Congressional and business leaders and arts and entertainment personalities. Further work experiences later took him to Tahiti and California where he catered for the motion picture industry in television and feature film.

Mr. Trebilcox has found a home at the A Bar A Ranch where he can showcase his talents while in a teaching environment. This is his first effort at a published work and comes as a result of much interest generated at the A Bar A by the many guests who return year after year to enjoy the meals created by the author and his staff.

Mr. Trebilcox shares time between homes in Virginia and Wyoming.

TO ORDER BOOKS

Copies are available from **The StoveArts Press**

The A BAR A Cookbook $10.95

Plus shipping, up to 3 books   2.50
[Over 3, add $1.00 per book]

Va. Residents add 4½% tax

Please send a check or money order to:

**The StoveArts Press
P.O. Box 7013
Dept. 101
Charlottesville, Va. 22906**

Comments and questions are welcome
Write to the author at the publisher's address or E Mail at
Ranchef @ Compuserve.com

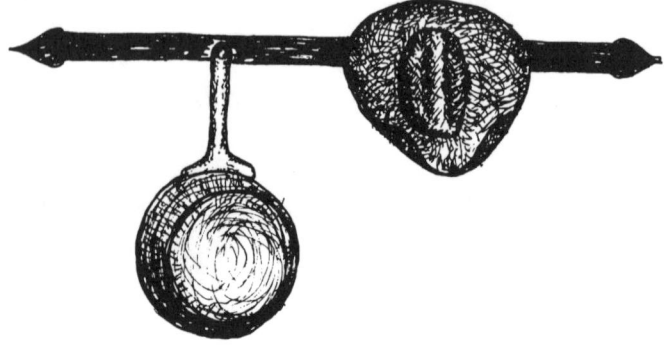